NVA STUDIOS

100 Iconic Concept Cars with Unique and Innovative Design

Copyright © 2023 by NVA STUDIOS

All rights reserved. No part of this publication may be reproduced, stored or transmitted in any form or by any means, electronic, mechanical, photocopying, recording, scanning, or otherwise without written permission from the publisher. It is illegal to copy this book, post it to a website, or distribute it by any other means without permission.

First edition

This book was professionally typeset on Reedsy. Find out more at reedsy.com

Contents

1	1935 Bugatti Aerolithe Concept	1
2	1938 Buick Y-Job	4
3	1954 Alfa Romeo BAT 7	7
4	1956 Ford Thunderbird Mexico	10
5	1966 Lamborghini Miura	13
6	1967 Mazda Cosmo 110S	16
7	1968 Alfa Romeo 33 Carabo	19
8	1968 Chevrolet Astro II	22
9	1969 Mercedes-Benz C111	25
10	1970 Ferrari 512S Modulo	28
11	1970 Lancia Stratos Zero	31
12	1970 Citroën SM	34
13	1970 Porsche Tapiro	37
14	1970 Chevrolet Corvette XP-882	40
15	1971 Lamborghini Countach LP500	44
16	1973 BMW 2002 Turbo	47
17	1975 Lotus Eclat	50
18	1978 Jaguar XJ Spider	54
19	1980 Aston Martin Bulldog	58
20	1980 Lamborghini Athon	61
21	1984 Peugeot Quasar	64
22	1984 Pontiac Fiero Concept	67
23	1985 Subaru XT Coupe	70
24	1986 Lamborghini LM002	73
25	1987 Oldsmobile Aerotech	76
26	1987 Chevrolet Express Concept	79

27	1987 Nissan Saurus	82
28	1990 Chevrolet Corvette CERV III	85
29	1990 BMW Z18	88
30	1991 Mazda 787B Concept	91
31	1992 Ford Ghia Focus Concept	94
32	1993 Aston Martin DB7 V12 Prototype TWR	97
33	1993 Mercedes-Benz Vision A93	101
34	1995 Ford GT90	105
35	1995 Toyota MRJ Concept	108
36	1996 Mercedes-Benz F200	111
37	1999 Cadillac Evoq	114
38	1999 Bugatti Veyron Concept	117
39	2000 Audi Rosemeyer	120
40	2001 Chrysler Crossfire	123
41	2001 Nissan GT-R Concept	126
42	2001 Honda NSX-R Concept	129
43	2002 Lexus 2054	132
44	2003 Ford GT40	135
45	2003 Cadillac Sixteen	138
46	2003 Mercedes F 500 Mind	141
47	2004 Peugeot 907	144
48	2005 Lexus LF-A Concept	147
49	2006 Lamborghini Miura Concept	151
50	2006 Saab Aero-X Concept	154
51	2007 BMW Concept CS	157
52	2008 Cadillac CTS Coupe Concept	160
53	2009 Aston Martin One-77 Prototype	163
54	2009 Chevrolet Corvette Stingray Concept	166
55	2010 Jaguar C-X75	169
56	2010 Audi Quattro Concept	172
57	2011 Chevrolet Miray Concept	175
58	2011 BMW i8 Concept	178
59	2011 Mercedes-Benz Silver Lightning	182

60	2012 Lexus LF-LC Concept	185
61	2012 Honda NSX Concept	188
62	2013 Nissan IDx	191
63	2013 Mercedes-Benz AMG Vision Gran Turismo	194
64	2014 Toyota FT-1	197
65	2014 Chevrolet Chaparral 2X Vision Gran Turismo	200
66	2015 Bugatti Vision Gran Turismo	203
67	2015 Porsche Mission E	207
68	2015 Aston Martin DBX Concept	210
69	2015 Hyundai N 2025 Vision Gran Turismo	213
70	2015 Mercedes-Benz F 015 Luxury in Motion	216
71	2016 MINI Vision Next 100	219
72	2016 BMW Vision Next 100	222
73	2016 Rolls-Royce Vision Next 100	226
74	2016 Cadillac Escala	229
75	2016 Lucid Air Concept	232
76	2017 Lamborghini Terzo Millennio	235
77	2017 BMW 8 Series Concept	238
78	2017 Honda Urban EV Concept	242
79	2017 Aston Martin Valkyrie	245
80	2017 Volkswagen ID. BUZZ Concept	249
81	2017 McLaren Ultimate Vision GT	252
82	2017 Nissan V-Motion 2.0	254
83	2017 Audi Aicon	257
84	2017 Lexus LS+ Concept	260
85	2018 Audi PB18 e-tron	263
86	2018 Mercedes-Benz Vision EQ Silver Arrow	267
87	2018 McLaren Speedtail	270
88	2018 Rivian R1S Concept	274
89	2019 Lamborghini V12 Vision Gran Turismo	277
90	2019 Mercedes-Benz Vision EQS	280
91	2019 Lexus LF-30 Electrified	283
92	2019 BMW Vision M Next	286

93	2019 Nissan Aria Concept	289
94	2019 Aston Martin Valhalla Prototype	292
95	2019 Canoo Lifestyle Vehicle Concept	295
96	2019 Bentley EXP 100 GT	298
97	2020 Mercedes-Benz Vision AVTR	301
98	2021 Audi RS Q e-tron	304
99	2021 Genesis X Concept	307
100	2021 Audi Skysphere	310

1

1935 Bugatti Aerolithe Concept

Picture a car that seems to have been crafted from moonlight and starshine, a vehicle so breathtakingly elegant that it borders on the surreal. This is the Bugatti Aerolithe Concept, a work of automotive artistry that harkens back to a bygone era while propelling us into the future.

The Bugatti Aerolithe Concept made its debut in 1935 at the Paris Auto Salon, and it was nothing short of a sensation. Designed by Jean Bugatti, the son of the company's founder Ettore Bugatti, this concept car was a showcase of both visionary design and innovative engineering.

One of the most captivating aspects of the Aerolithe was its bodywork, which was constructed from a magnesium alloy called Elektron. This material was not only incredibly lightweight but also had a radiant, silvery appearance that gave the car an otherworldly quality, hence the name "Aerolithe" which means "meteor" in French. The car's teardrop shape and the seamless flow of its curves were like a sculpture in motion, and it remains a symbol of automotive design excellence.

But the Aerolithe was not just a pretty face; it was also technologically advanced for its time. Under the hood lay a supercharged 3.3-liter inline-eight engine, which generated an impressive 140 horsepower. This power, coupled with the car's lightweight construction, allowed it to achieve remarkable speeds, pushing the boundaries of what was possible in the 1930s.

Despite its groundbreaking design and performance, the Bugatti Aerolithe was never intended for mass production. Only a single prototype was ever built, and it remains one of the most elusive and mysterious cars in automotive history. Legend has it that the original Aerolithe vanished without a trace after being exhibited at the Paris Auto Salon, adding an aura of mystique to its story.

However, the Aerolithe's legacy lives on. Its design elements, such as the teardrop shape and the use of lightweight materials, have influenced countless automotive designers over the years. Bugatti itself paid tribute to this iconic concept car with the Bugatti Veyron, a production supercar that incorporated many of the Aerolithe's design principles and performance aspirations.

In the world of concept cars, the Bugatti Aerolithe remains an eternal star—a symbol of artistic vision, daring innovation, and the relentless pursuit of automotive perfection. It reminds us that in the realm of automotive design, dreams have no limits, and the future is limited only by the imagination of those who dare to dream.

2

1938 Buick Y-Job

Step into the realm of automotive imagination, where innovation is an art and cars are the canvases. In this enchanting tale of innovation, the spotlight shines on the Buick Y-Job – a visionary concept car that not only defied its time but also shaped the very essence of modern automobiles.

Imagine the year 1938: an era of daring dreams and uncharted territories.

1938 BUICK Y-JOB

The Buick Y-Job emerges as a testament to the boundless creativity of its makers, a symphony conducted by the design genius of Harley Earl, the visionary behind General Motors' Art and Colour section. This masterful creation, a testament to the ingenuity of Buick, transcended the boundaries of what a car could be.

The Y-Job was a revolutionary statement of design philosophy, an embodiment of "longer, lower, wider" that would come to define the future of automobile aesthetics. Its sleek, streamlined form was a dance with the wind, sculpted not merely to cut through the air but to evoke emotion and capture the essence of movement even while standing still. Its presence hinted at the promise of speed, adventure, and the thrill of the open road.

But the Y-Job's prowess wasn't skin-deep. It dared to introduce innovations that would later become staples of modern automobiles. As its elegant exterior hinted at what lay beneath, its innovative heart unveiled features that seemed plucked from science fiction. Electric windows that whispered effortlessly, hidden headlights that blinked into existence at the touch of a button, and a power-operated convertible top that felt like the hand of destiny itself – the Y-Job was a glimpse into a utopian future of automotive luxury.

The magic didn't stop with its release; its influence rippled through time and transformed the very DNA of the automobile industry. Elements of the Y-Job's design vocabulary seeped into the veins of mass-produced cars, breathing life into vehicles that adorned the streets of the world. The idea of the "concept car" was born with the Y-Job, influencing the industry's landscape and propelling designers and engineers to continually push the boundaries of what was possible.

Released in 1938, the Buick Y-Job's impact echoes even today. It beckons us to dream beyond the constraints of the ordinary, to embrace innovation as a manifestation of human imagination. Its legacy extends beyond its years, whispering that even the grandest of visions can be realized with dedication, creativity, and the audacity to challenge conventions.

So, as you think of the Buick Y-Job, let it remind you that the road to progress is paved with audacious dreams and daring designs. Let its story be a testament to the fact that within every curve, every innovation, and every concept, lies the potential to shape the future of how we move, how we explore, and how we envision what lies beyond the horizon.

3

1954 Alfa Romeo BAT 7

Step into the world where art and innovation coalesce, where the lines between reality and imagination blur, and where the Alfa Romeo BAT 7 awaits to astound you. In the tapestry of automotive history, this iconic concept car stands as a testament to the marriage of breathtaking design and groundbreaking technology.

Picture yourself in the year 1954 – a time when the automotive landscape was ripe for a revolution. Enter the Alfa Romeo BAT 7, a creation born from the depths of both beauty and innovation. The BAT series (short for Berlina Aerodinamica Tecnica) was a triumphant collaboration between Alfa Romeo and the renowned design house Bertone, led by the visionary Franco Scaglione. But it was BAT 7 that emerged as the pinnacle of this partnership, a symphony of aerodynamic artistry and forward-thinking engineering.

The BAT 7's design is an ode to the marriage of form and function. Its body is a testament to the windswept allure of a teardrop, with curves that carve the air itself. The sleek, elongated silhouette and the mesmerizingly smooth surfaces are not just aesthetically captivating; they're a dance with the laws of aerodynamics. The prominent fins that adorn the rear of the car are not mere adornments; they are the embodiment of the fusion between art and science, a homage to the quest for efficiency and grace.

Beneath this stunning exterior beats a heart of innovation. The BAT 7 was designed with a focus on reducing air resistance – a pursuit that culminated in its drag coefficient being one of the lowest of its time. The car's unique, retractable headlights, flush with the body when not in use, showcased an integration of design and function that was years ahead of its time. Its groundbreaking technologies were not just fleeting novelties; they offered a glimpse into the future of automotive engineering.

1954 ALFA ROMEO BAT 7

The Alfa Romeo BAT 7 was unveiled to the world in 1954, an era when car design was finding its way into the hearts of the masses. Its influence, however, wasn't just confined to the niche world of concept cars. The principles it championed – the fusion of artistic aesthetics and technological innovation – seeped into the DNA of future production cars. The BAT series inspired automakers across the globe to embrace the concept of streamlined design and to weave technological prowess seamlessly into the fabric of every vehicle.

As you cast your imagination back to the year 1954 and envision the Alfa Romeo BAT 7, let it ignite your own aspirations. Let it remind you that in the pursuit of greatness, beauty and innovation are not adversaries, but allies. Just as the BAT 7 dared to dream beyond the conventional, so too can you dream beyond limits, guided by the understanding that even the most audacious ideas have the power to shape reality.

4

1956 Ford Thunderbird Mexico

Step into the realm where automotive dreams intertwine with a rich heritage, and let the story of the Ford Thunderbird Mexico sweep you away. In the tapestry of automotive history, this iconic concept car stands as a bridge between the past and the future, a testament to innovation that reverberates far beyond its wheels.

Imagine the year 1956, a time when the world was bustling with change and discovery. In the heart of this transformative era, the Ford Thunderbird Mexico emerged, not merely as a car, but as an embodiment of heritage, speed, and the spirit of exploration. Created by the visionaries at Ford, this concept car paid homage to the legendary Panamericana road race that had captured the imaginations of speed enthusiasts.

The Thunderbird Mexico's design is a mesmerizing blend of elegance and power. Its sleek lines pay tribute to the classic Thunderbirds of the past, while its elongated hood hints at the potential of a spirited drive. The car's color palette, a fusion of white and blue, is a nod to the Mexican flag and the Panamericana race that inspired its creation. From its sculpted body to its bold grille, every element was meticulously crafted to evoke a sense of motion even while stationary.

Beneath its exterior, the Thunderbird Mexico harbored innovative technologies that hinted at the future of automotive engineering. It boasted a powerful V8 engine that echoed the spirit of competition, capable of propelling the car to exhilarating speeds. Its streamlined form was designed not just for aesthetic allure but to cut through the air with precision, blending style and functionality in perfect harmony.

In 1956, the Ford Thunderbird Mexico was unveiled, capturing the imagination of all who laid eyes upon it. But its influence didn't stop there. The spirit of innovation and homage it embodied resonated with automakers and enthusiasts alike, sparking a renewed appreciation for heritage-infused design and performance. Elements of its aesthetic and technological advancements gradually found their way into the DNA of mass-produced cars, shaping the trajectory of the industry.

As you envision the Ford Thunderbird Mexico, let it be a reminder that the past and the future are not disparate realms, but interconnected narratives that weave the fabric of progress. Let it inspire you to blend tradition with innovation, to honor heritage while embracing the limitless possibilities of tomorrow. Just as the Thunderbird Mexico bridged eras, so too can you bridge aspirations and reality, guided by the understanding that even a single vehicle can ignite a revolution that reverberates for generations to come.

5

1966 Lamborghini Miura

Enter a realm where the roar of engines harmonizes with the poetry of design, where speed and artistry meld to create a symphony that echoes through time. In this world, the Lamborghini Miura reigns as a living legend, a concept car that transcended expectations and set the stage for the evolution of automotive excellence.

Imagine the mid-1960s, an era of rebellion and revolution, where traditional norms were being shattered in every corner. It's within this era of daring dreams that the Lamborghini Miura emerges, a creation that defied the boundaries of what a sports car could be. This concept car, born from the genius of Ferruccio Lamborghini and his visionary team, was not just a vehicle; it was a symbol of automotive audacity.

The Miura's design is a mesmerizing marriage of sensuality and power. Its sleek, low-slung profile exudes an air of predatory grace, a testament to the Italian artisans who sculpted it. The car's mid-engine layout wasn't just a technical choice; it was a declaration of Lamborghini's commitment to performance and balance. Every curve and contour of the Miura's body was not just a visual feast but a calculated dance with aerodynamics.

But the Miura wasn't just a beauty queen; it harbored technological innovations that set new standards. The heart of this beast was a transversely mounted V12 engine, a configuration that challenged conventions and laid the foundation for Lamborghini's future supercars. This innovative approach allowed for a compact design while delivering unparalleled power. The Miura wasn't just a concept car; it was a canvas upon which engineering marvels were painted.

In 1966, the Lamborghini Miura burst onto the scene, leaving the world breathless. Its influence, however, was far from fleeting. The Miura was more than a concept; it was a catalyst for Lamborghini's transformation from a manufacturer of luxury grand tourers to an icon of high-performance supercars. Its innovative engineering principles, from the mid-engine layout to the V12 powerplant, echoed through the marque's lineup, defining the essence of Lamborghini's spirit.

As you conjure the image of the Lamborghini Miura, let it be a reminder that the pursuit of greatness knows no limits. Just as this concept car shattered norms and ignited a revolution, so too can you break free from conventions and redefine your own horizons. The Miura's legacy isn't just in its breathtaking design or revolutionary technology; it's a testament that audacious dreams, when pursued with unrelenting passion, have the power to shape the world in ways that reverberate through generations.

6

1967 Mazda Cosmo 110S

Step into a world where innovation meets artistry, where the symphony of design and technology harmonize to create a masterpiece that defies the boundaries of the ordinary. In the heart of this realm stands the Mazda Cosmo 110S, a concept car that transformed dreams into reality, and set a course for a future where imagination reigns supreme.

Imagine the year 1967, an era marked by exploration and an unquenchable thirst for the unknown. It is within this era of boundless possibilities that the Mazda Cosmo 110S emerged, a creation that sprung from the imaginative minds at Mazda. This concept car was not merely a vehicle; it was a testament to Mazda's relentless pursuit of innovation and its unwavering commitment to pushing the boundaries of design and performance.

The Cosmo 110S's design is a marriage of elegance and avant-garde thinking. Its sleek, futuristic form is a declaration of Mazda's dedication to cutting-edge aesthetics. The graceful lines flow effortlessly, capturing the essence of motion even when standing still. The iconic rotary engine, Mazda's technological signature, found its place at the heart of the car, a reminder that this vehicle wasn't just a design marvel but a mechanical wonder as well.

Beneath its stylish exterior, the Mazda Cosmo 110S harbored a revolutionary powertrain. The rotary engine, a marvel of engineering, delivered not only impressive performance but also efficiency that defied convention. This engine's compact size and unique characteristics allowed it to generate substantial power while minimizing the weight of the vehicle, a concept that would reverberate through Mazda's future production cars.

In 1967, the Mazda Cosmo 110S took its grand stage, captivating the world with its futuristic allure. Its influence, however, reached far beyond its unveiling. The Cosmo 110S heralded the birth of Mazda's rotary engine technology, which would come to define the brand's identity and set it apart in the realm of automotive innovation. The concepts and lessons learned from this pioneering concept car would trickle down to Mazda's production vehicles, shaping their performance and fuel efficiency.

As you conjure the image of the Mazda Cosmo 110S, let it be a beacon of inspiration. Let it remind you that within the realms of creativity and innovation, there are no limits. Just as this concept car boldly embraced the unknown, so too can you embark on your own journey of exploration and innovation. The legacy of the Cosmo 110S isn't just in its revolutionary design and technology; it's a reminder that the fusion of imagination and engineering can transform mere dreams into tangible reality, shaping the road ahead for generations to come.

7

1968 Alfa Romeo 33 Carabo

Step into a world where dreams take shape in the form of machines, where innovation is an art, and where the Alfa Romeo 33 Carabo stands as a testament to the boundless creativity of human ingenuity. In this realm, the lines between possibility and reality blur, and a concept car becomes a tangible embodiment of tomorrow's aspirations.

Imagine the mid-1960s, an era marked by societal transformation and unbridled innovation. It is within this canvas of change that the Alfa Romeo 33 Carabo makes its entrance – a creation that not only defied conventions but rewrote the rules of automotive design. Born from the brilliant minds at Bertone, this concept car is more than metal and glass; it's a testament to the very spirit of pushing boundaries.

The Carabo's design is a striking fusion of form and function. Its wedge-shaped profile, reminiscent of a futuristic spacecraft, is not just a visual delight but an ode to aerodynamics. The scissor doors, a daring touch that would become an icon, are not just a stylistic choice but a declaration of the unconventional. The vibrant green hue, more than just a color, is a reflection of Alfa Romeo's racing heritage and a bold statement of individuality.

But the Carabo's essence is more than skin-deep; it's a playground of innovation. Beneath its exotic exterior, the Carabo hides an impressive technical arsenal. Its mechanicals were a tribute to Alfa Romeo's engineering prowess, with a V8 engine positioned behind the cockpit, setting the stage for future supercars. Innovative features like pop-up headlights and aero elements weren't just novelties; they were glimpses into the future of automotive technology.

In 1968, the Alfa Romeo 33 Carabo graced the world stage, leaving an indelible mark on the automotive landscape. Its influence, however, didn't fade with time; it catalyzed the evolution of design and engineering in ways that are felt even today. The Carabo's bold shapes and innovative features served as a harbinger of things to come, influencing generations of vehicles across various brands and segments.

As you envision the Alfa Romeo 33 Carabo, let it be a source of inspiration. Let it remind you that the road to innovation is often paved with audacity and a willingness to challenge norms. Just as the Carabo defied convention and sculpted its own path, so too can you carve your own trajectory in pursuit of your dreams. Its legacy isn't just a page in history; it's a reminder that human creativity knows no bounds, and that the seemingly unattainable can be transformed into tangible reality with passion, vision, and the courage to push beyond the ordinary.

8

1968 Chevrolet Astro II

Step into a world where imagination takes form in steel and glass, where innovation is the brush and the Chevrolet Astro II is the canvas. In this realm of automotive dreams, the Astro II stands as a testament to the power of creativity, a concept car that dares to imagine a future where design transcends the ordinary.

Imagine the vibrant 1960s, a time of change and boundless curiosity. Against this backdrop of cultural evolution, the Chevrolet Astro II makes its entrance, a creation that speaks volumes about the American spirit of innovation. This concept car, a brainchild of General Motors' design team, is more than a mere vehicle; it's a symbol of the desire to stretch the boundaries of what's possible.

The Astro II's design is a symphony of lines and curves, a marriage of sleekness and audacity. Its low-slung profile and aerodynamic contours are not just aesthetic choices but a testament to the understanding of airflow and speed. The canopy-like cockpit, with its expansive glass surfaces, beckons the future. The bold use of bright red, a hue that exudes energy and passion, underscores the car's embodiment of the 1960s spirit.

Yet, the Astro II's true magic lies within its technological innovations. Beneath its stunning exterior, this concept car housed a V8 engine that roared with power. Its experimental aerodynamics showcased the automotive industry's growing understanding of the importance of reducing drag for enhanced performance. The Astro II was more than just a design showcase; it was a playground for testing ideas that would shape the future of automobile engineering.

In 1968, the Chevrolet Astro II graced the world stage, capturing the imagination of all who beheld it. Its influence, however, echoed far beyond its initial unveiling. The lessons learned from its design and engineering impacted the trajectory of mass production vehicles. Its streamlined form and aerodynamic insights trickled down into everyday cars, reshaping the way manufacturers approached the balance between style and efficiency.

As you conjure the image of the Chevrolet Astro II, let it inspire you to embrace innovation and the daring spirit of exploration. Just as this concept car dared to imagine and push boundaries, so too can you venture into uncharted territories of your own aspirations. The Astro II's legacy isn't just confined to its futuristic form or cutting-edge technologies; it's a reminder that even the boldest visions can become reality with determination, creativity, and the willingness to leap beyond the ordinary.

9

1969 Mercedes-Benz C111

Step into a world where innovation is a guiding star and design is an ever-unfolding canvas. In this realm of automotive dreams, the Mercedes-Benz C111 emerges as a beacon of boundless imagination, a concept car that breaks barriers and whispers of a future where engineering and artistry unite.

Imagine the pulsating 1960s, a time of cultural revolution and scientific exploration. Amidst this backdrop of change, the Mercedes-Benz C111 graces the scene – a creation that is as much a testament to technological prowess as it is to the spirit of pushing limits. Born from the visionary minds at Mercedes-Benz, this concept car embodies a philosophy of embracing the uncharted and daring to envision the impossible.

The C111's design is an embodiment of fluid lines and futuristic vision, a masterpiece of aerodynamics that captivates the eye. Its low-slung, elongated body slices through the air with grace, hinting at the high-speed capabilities concealed within. The gull-wing doors, a nod to innovation and a dash of nostalgia, are not just a stylistic choice; they are a declaration of Mercedes-Benz's commitment to the marriage of form and function.

Yet, the C111's significance transcends its mesmerizing exterior. Beneath the skin lies a symphony of groundbreaking technologies that redefine what's feasible. The use of a Wankel rotary engine was revolutionary, offering compact power with a smooth delivery. The chassis incorporated lightweight materials and innovative suspension systems, setting new standards for performance and handling.

1969 MERCEDES-BENZ C111

In the late 1960s, the Mercedes-Benz C111 made its grand entrance, captivating the world with its futuristic allure. Its influence, however, was far-reaching. The C111's revolutionary approach to engine technology and materials paved the way for advancements in mass production vehicles. Its ethos of pushing boundaries and embracing innovation inspired engineers and designers to rethink conventions and explore new horizons.

As you envision the Mercedes-Benz C111, let it inspire you to venture beyond the confines of the known and embrace the allure of the unexplored. Let it be a reminder that the road to progress is often paved with curiosity and the willingness to take risks. Just as the C111's Wankel engine and innovative chassis influenced the future of automobile technology, so too can your own innovative spirit shape the world around you. The C111's legacy isn't just in its captivating design or pioneering technologies; it's a testament to the idea that the most extraordinary feats are born from the harmony of imagination, engineering, and the audacity to dream beyond limits.

10

1970 Ferrari 512S Modulo

Step into a world where innovation transcends the boundaries of tradition, where design is an art that pushes the limits of the imagination. In this realm of automotive wonder, the Ferrari 512S Modulo stands as a testament to the boundless creativity that can be ignited by the marriage of engineering and artistic expression.

Imagine the mid-1970s, a time of artistic revolution and technological curiosity. Amidst this tapestry of change, the Ferrari 512S Modulo emerges, a creation that defies the ordinary and redefines the concept of a car. Conceived by the visionary designer Paolo Martin for Pininfarina, this concept car embodies the very spirit of pushing boundaries and thinking beyond conventions.

The Modulo's design is an architectural marvel on wheels, a symphony of angles and surfaces that challenges the norms of automotive aesthetics. Its low, flat profile resembles a spacecraft from the future, echoing the era's fascination with space exploration. The wraparound windshield seamlessly integrates with the canopy-like roof, creating an uninterrupted vista for the driver. The bold red hue, synonymous with Ferrari's racing heritage, underlines the car's connection to performance.

But the Modulo's significance lies far beneath its mesmerizing exterior. This concept car was built on a Ferrari 512S chassis, a marriage of power and design that was unprecedented at the time. The cockpit, accessed by a sliding canopy, was designed to offer optimal visibility and control. The driver's seat was fixed, while the pedals and steering wheel adjusted to accommodate the driver – a testament to the ergonomic considerations that went into the Modulo's creation.

In 1970, the Ferrari 512S Modulo made its striking debut, capturing the world's attention with its futuristic allure. Its influence, however, extends beyond its unveiling. The Modulo's avant-garde design and focus on streamlined aerodynamics inspired elements that found their way into the design languages of subsequent supercars. Its radical interpretation of form and function pushed the envelope of what was possible, setting the stage for future generations of automotive innovation.

As you visualize the Ferrari 512S Modulo, let it kindle your own flames of innovation and creativity. Let it remind you that the road to greatness often requires daring to step into uncharted territory, where the extraordinary is born from the collaboration between imagination and engineering. The Modulo's legacy isn't merely confined to its distinctive design or technological marvels; it's a testament that even the wildest of visions can become reality when nurtured by passion, persistence, and the audacity to push beyond the ordinary.

11

1970 Lancia Stratos Zero

Step into a world where the boundaries of possibility dissolve, and design becomes a daring adventure. In this realm of automotive imagination, the Lancia Stratos Zero emerges as a beacon of innovation, a concept car that embodies the very essence of pushing the limits and embracing the unconventional.

Picture the free-spirited 1970s – an era of rebellion and innovation. Within this tapestry of change, the Lancia Stratos Zero takes its place, a creation that defies gravity and redefines the concept of an automobile. Crafted by the ingenious Marcello Gandini of Bertone, this concept car transcends the mundane, inviting us to explore the intersection of art and engineering.

The Stratos Zero's design is a feat of architectural audacity, an ode to geometric elegance that blurs the line between sculpture and vehicle. Its wedge-shaped silhouette defies gravity, as if it were a blade cutting through time. The glass canopy curves seamlessly into the sharply angled hood, creating an uninterrupted panorama for the driver. The futuristic orange hue, vibrant and electric, encapsulates the car's spirit of pushing the boundaries.

Yet, the Stratos Zero's significance extends beyond its visual impact. This concept car's purpose was not just to be admired but to challenge conventions. Its low, flattened stance highlighted the potential of aerodynamics in enhancing performance. It showcased the potential of unconventional designs to influence efficiency and handling, a revelation that would eventually find its way into the mass production cars of the future.

1970 LANCIA STRATOS ZERO

In 1970, the Lancia Stratos Zero made its spectacular debut, capturing imaginations with its daring design. Its influence, however, is far-reaching. The Stratos Zero's bold angles and futuristic aesthetics served as an inspiration for generations of car designers, influencing the angular design trends of the 1970s and beyond. Its philosophy of merging form and function set a precedent for vehicles that prioritized both aesthetics and performance.

As you envision the Lancia Stratos Zero, let it be a source of inspiration to venture beyond the conventional and embrace the uncharted. Let it remind you that innovation often lies at the intersection of art and technology. Just as the Stratos Zero dared to reimagine the limits of design, so too can you redefine the boundaries of your own aspirations. Its legacy isn't confined to its stunning design or engineering innovations; it's a reminder that the most remarkable achievements arise from the fusion of creativity, courage, and the audacity to challenge the status quo.

12

1970 Citroën SM

Step into a realm where innovation and artistry intertwine, where a single car becomes a symphony of design and engineering. In this world of automotive dreams, the Citroën SM emerges as a mesmerizing masterpiece, a concept car that breaks free from convention and propels us into the realm of boundless

1970 CITROËN SM

possibility.

Imagine the 1970s, a time of cultural evolution and technological exploration. Amidst this backdrop of change, the Citroën SM graces the scene – a creation that defies categorization and challenges the very essence of what a car can be. Born from the visionary minds of Citroën, this concept car embodies a philosophy of pushing boundaries and redefining the status quo.

The SM's design is a ballet of curves and angles, an embodiment of futuristic elegance that beckons us to imagine a world beyond the ordinary. Its long, sleek silhouette exudes an air of sophistication, while its innovative aerodynamics hint at the marriage of form and function. The large, streamlined headlights are not just a visual statement; they're an homage to the car's innovative lighting technology that set new standards for the era.

But the SM's significance extends beyond its captivating exterior. Underneath the surface, it harbored groundbreaking technologies that were years ahead of its time. The hydro-pneumatic suspension system, a signature of Citroën, offered unparalleled comfort and handling. The Maserati-sourced V6 engine combined performance and refinement, a synergy that redefined expectations for a luxury grand tourer.

In 1970, the Citroën SM made its entrance, leaving the world entranced by its futuristic allure. Its influence, however, didn't stop with its unveiling. The SM's fusion of design and technology served as a beacon for the industry, influencing the direction of luxury cars. Elements of its advanced suspension and innovative lighting technology found their way into mass production vehicles, shaping the way manufacturers approached comfort and safety.

As you visualize the Citroën SM, let it be a reminder to embrace the beauty of innovation and the audacity to push the limits of what's possible. Just as this concept car dared to blur the lines between luxury and performance, so too can you transcend conventional boundaries in your pursuits. The SM's legacy isn't just in its striking design or pioneering technologies; it's a testament to the idea that the intersection of creativity and engineering can give rise to feats that transform the world and inspire us to reach for the stars.

13

1970 Porsche Tapiro

Imagine a world where the wind itself becomes a sculptor, molding the future of automotive design with its gentle touch. In this world of visionary creation, the Porsche Tapiro emerges as a work of art that defies the conventions of its time and ushers in a new era of aesthetic and technological exploration.

Step into the mid-1970s, a period marked by the pursuit of innovation and the promise of what's next. Amidst this backdrop of curiosity and change, the Porsche Tapiro graces the stage – a concept car that seems to have been hatched from the dreams of tomorrow. Crafted by the brilliant minds at ItalDesign, the Tapiro is more than a vehicle; it's an embodiment of Porsche's commitment to pushing the boundaries.

The Tapiro's design is a symphony of sleek lines and bold angles, a harmony of form and function that elicits a sense of awe. Its low-slung profile and futuristic canopy create an illusion of motion even when standing still. The scissor doors, more than just a nod to the avant-garde, evoke a sense of discovery and unveiling. The iridescent blue hue, reminiscent of the future's promise, reflects the car's audacious spirit.

Yet, the Tapiro's significance extends far beyond its arresting exterior. This concept car was a playground of innovations that set it apart as a visionary creation. Its turbocharged V8 engine harnessed power and efficiency, echoing Porsche's commitment to performance. The distinctive bodywork and advanced aerodynamics showcased a deep understanding of how form can elevate function, influencing the brand's design language for years to come.

1970 PORSCHE TAPIRO

In 1970, the Porsche Tapiro made its striking debut, leaving a trail of wonder in its wake. Its influence, however, didn't fade with time; it served as a touchstone for Porsche's exploration of design and engineering. The Tapiro's aerodynamic cues and turbocharged technology trickled down into the brand's mass production cars, shaping the direction of Porsche's performance-oriented lineup.

As you envision the Porsche Tapiro, let it fuel your own aspirations to embrace the unconventional and challenge the ordinary. Let it remind you that innovation often resides in the marriage of artistic vision and engineering ingenuity. Just as the Tapiro's groundbreaking design elements and technological marvels influenced Porsche's future, so too can your audacious pursuits shape the trajectory of your own journey. The Tapiro's legacy isn't confined to its exquisite design or pioneering technologies; it's a testament to the idea that the most extraordinary achievements arise from the intersection of creativity, determination, and the courage to venture into uncharted territory.

14

1970 Chevrolet Corvette XP-882

Imagine a realm where speed and elegance unite in a dance of innovation and artistry. In this world of automotive dreams, the Chevrolet Corvette XP-882 emerges as a symbol of design courage and engineering prowess, a concept car that reimagines the future of performance with audacity and grace.

1970 CHEVROLET CORVETTE XP-882

Step into the electrifying atmosphere of the 1970s, a time of transformation and daring visions. Against this backdrop of change, the Chevrolet Corvette XP-882 makes its grand entrance – a creation that dares to challenge conventions and rewrite the script of the American sports car. Born from the brilliance of Chevrolet's designers and engineers, this concept car embodies a philosophy of relentless pursuit of excellence.

The XP-882's design is a synthesis of sleekness and raw power, a manifestation of speed captured in a sculptural form. Its low, aggressive stance hints at the untamed energy that resides within. The sweeping lines and aerodynamic shapes evoke the sensation of movement, even at a standstill. The retractable headlights, like the eyes of a predator, are not just a design flourish; they are a testament to the XP-882's embrace of cutting-edge technology.

However, the XP-882's significance runs much deeper than its striking exterior. Underneath the surface lies a symphony of innovation. This concept car was the first to showcase the radical "Wankel" rotary engine, an engineering marvel that promised both power and efficiency. This revolutionary powerplant would go on to influence the direction of automotive technology, sparking conversations and advancements that echoed through the industry.

In 1973, the Chevrolet Corvette XP-882 made its dynamic debut, capturing the spirit of its era with its futuristic allure. Its influence, however, didn't end with its unveiling. The XP-882's daring approach to design and its introduction of new technologies set the stage for the future of sports cars. The concept's influence extended to other models within the Chevrolet lineup, sparking conversations about alternative powertrains and advanced engineering.

As you envision the Chevrolet Corvette XP-882, let it remind you of the power of embracing innovation and pushing boundaries. Let it be a beacon of inspiration for you to transcend the limits of convention and explore uncharted territories in your own pursuits. Just as the XP-882's groundbreaking technologies paved the way for future advancements, so too can your audacious endeavors ignite a ripple of transformation in your world. Its legacy isn't confined to its pioneering design or innovative engine; it's a testament to the idea that the fusion of creativity and engineering can shape the future and inspire us to reach for new horizons.

15

1971 Lamborghini Countach LP500

Imagine a world where dreams become reality, where the roar of engines harmonizes with the symphony of design. In this realm of automotive wonder, the Lamborghini Countach LP500 strides forward as a beacon of aspiration, a concept car that embodies the audacious spirit of pushing limits and crafting legends.

1971 LAMBORGHINI COUNTACH LP500

Step into the bold era of the 1970s, a time when the pursuit of excellence was matched only by the yearning for the extraordinary. Amidst this age of ambition, the Lamborghini Countach LP500 makes its captivating entrance – a creation that transcends mere machinery to become a symbol of innovation and beauty. Conceived by the visionary minds at Lamborghini, this concept car embodies a philosophy of fearless exploration and engineering brilliance.

The Countach LP500's design is a symphony of sharp angles and primal power, an embodiment of speed chiseled into form. Its low-slung, wedge-shaped silhouette cuts through the air with the precision of a razor blade. The scissor doors, akin to the wings of a mythical creature, offer a touch of drama to the act of unveiling. The vibrant orange hue, like the fire of creation, pays homage to Lamborghini's bold legacy.

Yet, the Countach LP500's significance reaches far beyond its arresting exterior. Under its aerodynamic skin beats the heart of innovation. This concept car introduced Lamborghini's revolutionary V12 engine, positioned behind the driver for optimal balance. Its engine's displacement – 5.0 liters – inspired the "LP500" in its name, setting the stage for Lamborghini's future legendary powerplants.

In 1971, the Lamborghini Countach LP500 dazzled the world with its futuristic allure. Its influence, however, continued to resonate long after its debut. The LP500's design language, characterized by its razor-sharp edges and bold lines, set the tone for Lamborghini's future supercars. Its groundbreaking engine placement and performance-oriented design philosophy reverberated through the brand's lineup, transforming it into a symbol of pure automotive passion.

As you conjure the image of the Lamborghini Countach LP500, let it remind you to embrace audacity and the unwavering pursuit of excellence. Let it inspire you to reach beyond the limits, to redefine what's possible. Just as the LP500's innovative engine and daring design choices paved the way for Lamborghini's legacy, so too can your audacious spirit shape your own path. Its legacy isn't confined to its stunning design or groundbreaking technology; it's a testament that the fusion of creativity, engineering, and courage can create masterpieces that inspire us to transcend the ordinary and write our own legendary stories.

16

1973 BMW 2002 Turbo

Step into a world where the road becomes a canvas and innovation is the artist's brush. In this realm of automotive creativity, the BMW 2002 Turbo emerges as a masterpiece that blurs the line between exhilaration and engineering. It's a concept car that ignites the spirit of driving and encapsulates the very essence of a brand's journey to push limits.

Picture the vibrant 1970s, an era marked by a thirst for speed and an appetite for style. Against this backdrop of enthusiasm, the BMW 2002 Turbo makes its dramatic entrance – a creation that doesn't just embody a brand's ethos but galvanizes the very soul of driving enthusiasts. Born from the spirited minds at BMW, this concept car epitomizes the pursuit of excellence.

The 2002 Turbo's design is a marriage of form and function, a symphony of lines that hint at the power within. Its compact and muscular silhouette exudes an air of sportiness, while the flared wheel arches pay homage to its racing pedigree. The bold "turbo" script on the rear, more than a mere emblem, is a declaration of its heart – a turbocharged engine that redefines performance.

But the 2002 Turbo's significance extends beyond its eye-catching exterior. Beneath the surface lies an array of innovative technologies that redefine what's possible. This concept car was the first European production car with a turbocharged engine, an engineering feat that transformed a compact car into a powerhouse of acceleration. The result was not just a surge in speed but a pioneering chapter in the history of turbocharging.

1973 BMW 2002 TURBO

In 1973, the BMW 2002 Turbo roared onto the scene, captivating hearts with its blend of style and performance. Its influence, however, reverberated far beyond its initial unveiling. The 2002 Turbo's success paved the way for the mass production of turbocharged cars, not only transforming the landscape of motorsports but also shaping the future of road-going vehicles. Its legacy wasn't just a footnote in history; it was a catalyst for the turbo revolution.

As you envision the BMW 2002 Turbo, let it ignite your own flames of ambition and innovation. Let it remind you that the road to excellence often requires embracing the uncharted and challenging the status quo. Just as the 2002 Turbo's turbocharged engine became a defining feature for generations of cars, so too can your own pioneering spirit shape the trajectory of your endeavors. Its legacy isn't confined to its captivating design or groundbreaking technology; it's a testament to the idea that the fusion of passion, engineering, and courage can reshape industries and inspire us to accelerate towards our dreams.

17

1975 Lotus Eclat

Step into a world where innovation and artistry merge to create an automotive symphony, where a car becomes a canvas of possibilities. In this realm of dynamic design, the Lotus Eclat emerges as a masterpiece that dares to harmonize performance and elegance in a single stroke.

1975 LOTUS ECLAT

Imagine the exhilarating 1970s, a time of freedom and exploration. Against this backdrop of change, the Lotus Eclat steps forward – a creation that not only captures the spirit of its era but redefines the notion of a grand tourer. Conceived by the ingenious minds at Lotus, this concept car epitomizes the brand's ethos of lightweight performance and technological ingenuity.

The Eclat's design is a fusion of grace and power, an embodiment of speed draped in sophistication. Its sleek, elongated silhouette exudes an air of exclusivity, while the sculpted lines emphasize its aerodynamic prowess. The large glass surfaces, seemingly endless, invite the outside world to become a part of the driving experience. The vibrant orange hue, like a sunrise on the horizon, symbolizes the dawn of a new era in automotive design.

But the Eclat's significance runs deeper than its mesmerizing exterior. Beneath its skin lies a symphony of innovation and engineering precision. This concept car embraced the brand's heritage of lightweight construction, blending performance with efficiency. Its mid-mounted engine allowed for optimal weight distribution, a feat that contributed to its exceptional handling and driving dynamics.

In 1975, the Lotus Eclat graced the world stage, capturing the imagination with its fusion of form and function. Its influence, however, extended beyond its initial unveiling. The Eclat's focus on balance, performance, and lightweight construction set a precedent for future Lotus models and influenced the brand's design philosophy for years to come. Its legacy isn't just confined to the realm of concept cars; it's an integral part of Lotus's journey toward creating iconic production vehicles.

As you visualize the Lotus Eclat, let it kindle your own flames of innovation and pursuit of excellence. Let it remind you that the road to greatness often requires embracing cutting-edge technologies and pushing the boundaries of design. Just as the Eclat's meticulous engineering and striking aesthetics influenced the trajectory of Lotus, so too can your own daring spirit shape the course of your ambitions. Its legacy isn't confined to its distinctive design or performance innovations; it's a testament to the idea that the convergence of creativity, engineering, and determination can create masterpieces that transcend the ordinary and inspire us to accelerate towards our dreams.

18

1978 Jaguar XJ Spider

Step into a world where elegance takes a bold leap into the realm of the unexpected, where innovation blooms in the most refined of settings. In this ethereal landscape of automotive design, the Jaguar XJ Spider emerges as a masterpiece that defies conventions and crafts a tale of sophistication and daring innovation.

1978 JAGUAR XJ SPIDER

Imagine the alluring era of the 1970s, a time when luxury and exploration danced in harmony. Amidst this tapestry of style and possibility, the Jaguar XJ Spider makes its grand entrance – a concept car that doesn't merely define luxury but elevates it to new heights. Born from the visionary minds at Jaguar, this concept car embodies the brand's commitment to pushing boundaries and rewriting the script of automotive aesthetics.

The XJ Spider's design is an ode to fluidity and grace, a symphony of lines that speak of movement even in stillness. Its elongated profile exudes an air of regality, while the sweeping curves and sculpted surfaces evoke the sensation of wind brushing against the skin. The open-top design, like an invitation to embrace the world around, allows the occupants to bask in the elements. The opulent shade of British Racing Green, reminiscent of Jaguar's heritage, adds a touch of nostalgia and prestige.

Yet, the XJ Spider's significance runs far deeper than its captivating exterior. Underneath its mesmerizing form resides a symphony of cutting-edge technology and innovation. This concept car served as a platform for showcasing new materials and construction techniques, a testament to Jaguar's commitment to engineering excellence. Its lightweight construction and powerful V12 engine combined to create an unparalleled driving experience.

In 1978, the Jaguar XJ Spider graced the world stage, capturing the imagination with its blend of luxury and performance. Its influence, however, reached beyond its initial unveiling. The XJ Spider's experimentation with materials and technologies seeped into Jaguar's production vehicles, shaping the brand's future approach to engineering and design. Its legacy isn't just a moment in history; it's a chapter in the ongoing story of innovation.

As you conjure the image of the Jaguar XJ Spider, let it be a source of inspiration to embrace the balance between tradition and innovation. Let it remind you that true greatness often requires the audacity to redefine the limits of elegance and technology. Just as the XJ Spider's pioneering spirit and advanced materials influenced the direction of Jaguar's production cars, so too can your own pursuit of excellence leave a lasting imprint on your journey. Its legacy isn't confined to its distinctive design or technological marvels; it's a testament to the idea that the fusion of creativity, engineering, and courage can create masterpieces that inspire us to accelerate towards

1978 JAGUAR XJ SPIDER

our dreams.

19

1980 Aston Martin Bulldog

Prepare to be transported to a world where automotive dreams know no bounds – where speed meets sculpture, and innovation dances with design. In the heart of this realm stands the Aston Martin Bulldog, a concept car that defies conventions and elevates the very essence of what a car can be.

Imagine the year 1980 – an era that embraced the horizon of the future with open arms. It's in this canvas of time that the Aston Martin Bulldog emerged, an embodiment of audaciousness and technical prowess. Aston Martin, renowned for its luxury grand tourers, dared to venture into uncharted territory, creating a concept car that would challenge the boundaries of speed and design.

The Bulldog's design is a symphony of aerodynamic elegance. Its low, wedge-shaped profile carves through the air with an almost otherworldly grace, hinting at the raw power that lies beneath. The expansive windshield wraps seamlessly into the roof, blurring the lines between car and cockpit. The gull-wing doors, akin to wings about to take flight, bestow an air of futuristic extravagance.

But the Bulldog's true innovation lay beneath its skin. This concept car was equipped with a mighty 5.3-liter twin-turbocharged V8 engine that roared with a thunderous 600 horsepower. It was a vision of performance that defied the era's standards. With a projected top speed of over 200 mph, the Bulldog was poised to shatter records and redefine the perception of speed in a road car.

In the year 1980, the Aston Martin Bulldog was unveiled, a dazzling spectacle that captivated the world. While this singular car remained a concept, its influence echoed through the corridors of automotive innovation. Its pursuit of speed inspired advancements in aerodynamics and engine technology, shaping the future of performance cars. Elements of its design language and technical marvels made their way into the DNA of production vehicles, ushering in a new era of performance-driven design.

As you conjure the image of the Aston Martin Bulldog, let it be a reminder that the pursuit of excellence knows no boundaries. Just as this concept car pushed the limits of what was thought possible, so too can you push the boundaries of your own aspirations. The Bulldog's legacy is not just in its groundbreaking design or blistering speed, but in its reminder that even in the realm of dreams, there's room for innovation, audacity, and the relentless pursuit of what lies beyond the horizon.

20

1980 Lamborghini Athon

Imagine a world where innovation knows no bounds, where a car becomes a canvas for the boldest of artistic visions. In this realm of automotive creativity, the Lamborghini Athon emerges as a symphony of design and technology that redefines what's possible on four wheels.

Step into the visionary 1980s, an era marked by a hunger for the extraordinary and a thirst for the avant-garde. Amidst this backdrop of aspiration, the Lamborghini Athon enters the scene – a concept car that dares to fuse luxury and power with an audacious spirit. Conceived by the imaginative minds at Lamborghini, this concept car epitomizes a philosophy of pushing limits and crafting rolling works of art.

The Athon's design is a fusion of curves and edges, a dance of elegance and aggression that commands attention. Its low, sculpted profile exudes an air of dynamic grace, while the pop-up headlights and gull-wing doors accentuate its futuristic allure. The seamless blend of glass and metal creates an uninterrupted panorama, inviting the outside world to become a part of the driving experience. The vibrant orange hue, like a sunburst on the horizon, captures Lamborghini's essence of daring and allure.

But the Athon's significance stretches far beyond its mesmerizing exterior. Under its skin lies a tapestry of innovation and engineering ingenuity. This concept car showcased Lamborghini's prowess in advanced materials and design, presenting a vision of the future where performance met sophistication. Its compact V8 engine exemplified power and efficiency, redefining the boundaries of a luxury sports car.

1980 LAMBORGHINI ATHON

In 1980, the Lamborghini Athon made its entrancing debut, capturing imaginations with its blend of form and function. Its influence, however, resonated far beyond its initial unveiling. The Athon's design cues and technological explorations found echoes in Lamborghini's later production vehicles, shaping the brand's approach to luxury and performance. Its legacy wasn't confined to the realm of concept cars; it was a catalyst for Lamborghini's journey into a new era.

As you envision the Lamborghini Athon, let it ignite your own aspirations to push boundaries and redefine the limits of creativity. Let it remind you that the path to greatness often requires embracing innovation and embracing the uncharted. Just as the Athon's pioneering design and advanced materials influenced Lamborghini's future, so too can your audacious spirit shape the course of your own journey. Its legacy isn't confined to its breathtaking design or groundbreaking technology; it's a testament to the idea that the fusion of passion, engineering, and courage can shape industries and inspire us to accelerate towards our dreams.

21

1984 Peugeot Quasar

Step into a realm where imagination meets innovation, where automotive design becomes a canvas for boundless creativity. In this world of visionary exploration, the Peugeot Quasar emerges as a masterpiece that transcends the ordinary and paints a vivid portrait of a future where design and technology dance in harmony.

Picture the electric atmosphere of the 1980s, an era defined by its hunger for progress and fascination with the unknown. Against this backdrop of change, the Peugeot Quasar enters the stage – a concept car that seems to be plucked from the realm of science fiction and brought to life. Conceived by the ingenious minds at Peugeot, this concept car encapsulates the brand's commitment to pushing boundaries and crafting a symphony of art and engineering.

The Quasar's design is an orchestration of angles and curves, a marriage of aesthetics and aerodynamics that captivates the eye. Its low-slung profile exudes an air of speed and innovation, while the geometric lines and precision detailing hint at its avant-garde spirit. The gull-wing doors, more than just an entrance, evoke a sense of unveiling and anticipation. The sleek metallic finish, like liquid silver, mirrors the car's essence of fluidity and brilliance.

Yet, the Quasar's significance extends far beyond its arresting exterior. Underneath the surface lies a symphony of innovation and technological exploration. This concept car embraced digital instrumentation and cutting-edge materials, showcasing Peugeot's vision of a future where technology harmonizes with design. Its mid-mounted V6 engine heralded performance and sophistication, a union that elevated the driving experience to new heights.

In 1984, the Peugeot Quasar made its dazzling debut, capturing imaginations with its fusion of aesthetics and innovation. Its influence, however, echoes long after its initial unveiling. The Quasar's design cues and technological marvels left an indelible mark on Peugeot's future production vehicles, shaping the brand's design language and engineering philosophy. Its legacy isn't confined to a single moment; it's a beacon that guides the brand's evolution.

As you conjure the image of the Peugeot Quasar, let it stir your own aspirations to blend creativity and technology in your pursuits. Let it remind you that the path to greatness often involves embracing the unexplored and challenging conventions. Just as the Quasar's groundbreaking design and innovative technologies influenced Peugeot's journey, so too can your own audacious spirit shape the trajectory of your dreams. Its legacy isn't confined to its striking design or technological marvels; it's a testament to the idea that the fusion of passion, engineering, and courage can create masterpieces that inspire us to accelerate towards our aspirations.

22

1984 Pontiac Fiero Concept

Enter a world where dreams transform into reality, where the line between imagination and innovation blurs. In this landscape of automotive creativity, the Pontiac Fiero Concept emerges as a beacon of bold design and visionary engineering, a car that not only pushes boundaries but reshapes the way we envision the future of transportation.

Picture the vibrant canvas of the 1980s, a period marked by a thirst for the extraordinary and a craving for the unconventional. Against this backdrop of change, the Pontiac Fiero Concept takes center stage – a creation that doesn't just redefine a brand's identity but ignites a revolution in automotive design. Conceived by the innovative minds at Pontiac, this concept car encapsulates a philosophy of fusing form and function into a harmonious masterpiece.

The Fiero Concept's design is a symphony of sleek lines and aggressive elegance, an embodiment of speed and sophistication that captivates the soul. Its low, aerodynamic profile exudes an air of power and grace, while the dramatic curves and bold detailing hint at its futuristic spirit. The retractable headlights, like the eyes of a visionary, unveil a glimpse into what lies ahead. The striking red hue, like a burst of passion, mirrors the car's essence of energy and innovation.

Yet, the Fiero Concept's significance stretches beyond its captivating exterior. Under its skin lies a realm of innovative technology and engineering marvels. This concept car showcased Pontiac's commitment to cutting-edge materials and performance. Its mid-engine layout not only redefined the driving experience but hinted at the future of sports car design. The concept car's experiments with aerodynamics and materials resonated in Pontiac's production cars, shaping the brand's future endeavors.

1984 PONTIAC FIERO CONCEPT

In 1984, the Pontiac Fiero Concept made its grand entrance, mesmerizing onlookers with its fusion of form and function. Its influence, however, transcended its initial unveiling. The Fiero Concept's design philosophy and technological explorations echoed through Pontiac's lineup, influencing the direction of the brand's vehicles. Its legacy isn't just confined to the concept car; it's a cornerstone in Pontiac's journey towards creating vehicles that inspire awe.

As you envision the Pontiac Fiero Concept, let it awaken your own aspirations to blend creativity and engineering in your pursuits. Let it remind you that progress often emerges from the convergence of vision and innovation. Just as the Fiero Concept's daring design and technological innovations influenced Pontiac's trajectory, so too can your own audacious spirit shape the course of your endeavors. Its legacy isn't confined to its breathtaking design or groundbreaking technology; it's a testament to the idea that the fusion of passion, engineering, and courage can shape industries and inspire us to accelerate towards our dreams.

23

1985 Subaru XT Coupe

Imagine a universe where the road becomes a canvas and engineering is the brush that paints the future. In this realm of automotive innovation, the Subaru XT Coupe emerges as a symphony of design and technology that defies convention and challenges our perceptions of what a car can be.

Visualize the dynamic landscape of the 1980s, an era characterized by bold exploration and a yearning for the avant-garde. Against this backdrop of change, the Subaru XT Coupe takes center stage – a concept car that doesn't just hint at the future but propels us into it. Conceived by the ingenious minds at Subaru, this concept car embodies a philosophy of pushing boundaries and crafting a harmony of style and performance.

The XT Coupe's design is an embodiment of sleekness and futuristic allure, a fusion of form and function that captures the imagination. Its low, aerodynamic profile exudes an air of speed and modernity, while the sculpted lines and pop-up headlights evoke a sense of excitement and anticipation. The distinctive angular design, like a sculpted work of art, challenges traditional notions of car aesthetics. The vibrant two-tone color scheme, like a burst of creativity, mirrors the car's essence of innovation and individuality.

Yet, the XT Coupe's significance stretches beyond its captivating exterior. Underneath its surface lies a world of pioneering technology and engineering ingenuity. This concept car introduced advanced features like a digital dashboard and an available turbocharged engine, hinting at Subaru's commitment to blending innovation with performance. The XT Coupe's daring design and technological experiments resonated in Subaru's production cars, influencing the brand's trajectory.

In 1985, the Subaru XT Coupe made its debut, capturing attention with its blend of style and innovation. Its influence, however, continued to resonate beyond its initial unveiling. The XT Coupe's design cues and technological marvels found their way into Subaru's future vehicles, shaping the brand's approach to design and technology. Its legacy isn't confined to the concept car; it's a driving force in Subaru's journey to create vehicles that inspire awe.

As you envision the Subaru XT Coupe, let it kindle your own flames of innovation and pursuit of excellence. Let it remind you that true greatness often involves embracing the uncharted and challenging conventions. Just as the XT Coupe's pioneering spirit and groundbreaking features influenced Subaru's trajectory, so too can your audacious endeavors shape the path of your own aspirations. Its legacy isn't just limited to its striking design or technological marvels; it's a testament to the idea that the fusion of passion, engineering, and courage can create masterpieces that inspire us to accelerate towards our dreams.

24

1986 Lamborghini LM002

Step into a realm where the road meets ruggedness, where power and luxury intertwine to create an automotive marvel. In this landscape of bold exploration, the Lamborghini LM002 emerges as a symbol of audacity and innovation, a concept car that defies convention and ushers in a new era of utility and extravagance.

Imagine the captivating 1980s, an era marked by a thirst for the extraordinary and a penchant for the adventurous. Amidst this tapestry of change, the Lamborghini LM002 makes its grand entrance – a creation that blurs the lines between opulence and off-road capability. Conceived by the visionary minds at Lamborghini, this concept car embodies a philosophy of pushing boundaries and crafting a fusion of power and prestige.

The LM002's design is a fusion of brute force and elegance, an embodiment of strength draped in luxury. Its imposing profile exudes an air of authority and ruggedness, while the bold lines and angular design evoke a sense of dominance. The boxy shape, like a fortress on wheels, hints at its off-road prowess. The gleaming paintwork, like a coat of armor, reflects Lamborghini's essence of grandeur and innovation.

Yet, the LM002's significance transcends its captivating exterior. Underneath its robust frame lies a realm of innovative technology and engineering brilliance. This concept car introduced the world to the idea of a high-performance luxury SUV, fusing Lamborghini's high-performance DNA with off-road capabilities. Its V12 engine roared with the same power found in Lamborghini's supercars, a testament to the brand's commitment to performance.

1986 LAMBORGHINI LM002

In 1986, the Lamborghini LM002 made its awe-inspiring debut, captivating imaginations with its blend of luxury and ruggedness. Its influence, however, resonated far beyond its initial unveiling. The LM002's audacious spirit and innovative approach to luxury and performance influenced the trajectory of future luxury SUVs, shaping the direction of the automotive industry.

As you conjure the image of the Lamborghini LM002, let it awaken your own spirit of audacity and exploration. Let it remind you that the journey to greatness often involves embracing the unexpected and challenging conventions. Just as the LM002's powerful performance and luxurious features influenced the course of luxury SUVs, so too can your own audacious spirit shape the trajectory of your own endeavors. Its legacy isn't confined to its commanding design or pioneering technology; it's a testament to the idea that the fusion of passion, engineering, and courage can create masterpieces that inspire us to accelerate towards our dreams.

25

1987 Oldsmobile Aerotech

Imagine a world where speed becomes a symphony and innovation is the conductor's baton. In this realm of automotive exploration, the Oldsmobile Aerotech emerges as a masterpiece that pushes the boundaries of velocity and engineering excellence. It's a concept car that not only embraces the pursuit of speed but redefines what's possible in the world of high-performance.

Picture the exhilarating 1980s, an era marked by a quest for velocity and the thrill of pushing limits. Against this backdrop of aspiration, the Oldsmobile Aerotech takes center stage — a creation that doesn't just break records but shatters expectations. Conceived by the visionary minds at Oldsmobile, this concept car embodies a philosophy of relentless pursuit and unwavering determination.

The Aerotech's design is a fusion of aerodynamics and aesthetics, a symphony of form and function that slices through the air with precision. Its low-slung profile exudes an air of speed and efficiency, while the sculpted lines and streamlined shape hint at its pursuit of aerodynamic perfection. The vibrant silver hue, like a comet streaking through the sky, captures the car's essence of motion and innovation.

Yet, the Aerotech's significance reaches beyond its captivating exterior. Underneath its sleek skin lies a realm of groundbreaking technology and engineering brilliance. This concept car introduced advanced aerodynamic principles and innovative materials, showcasing Oldsmobile's commitment to pushing the envelope of speed. Its high-performance engine and engineering innovations inspired future generations of high-speed vehicles.

In 1987, the Oldsmobile Aerotech made its dazzling debut, captivating imaginations with its blend of form and velocity. Its influence, however, extended far beyond its initial unveiling. The Aerotech's pioneering aerodynamic design and innovative technologies resonated in the automotive industry, shaping the way high-performance vehicles are engineered and designed.

As you conjure the image of the Oldsmobile Aerotech, let it spark your own aspirations to break barriers and redefine limits. Let it remind you that true greatness often involves embracing innovation and surpassing expectations. Just as the Aerotech's pursuit of speed and engineering breakthroughs influenced the trajectory of high-performance vehicles, so too can your own audacious spirit shape the course of your aspirations. Its legacy isn't confined to its cutting-edge design or pioneering technology; it's a testament to the idea that the fusion of passion, engineering, and courage can shape industries and inspire us to accelerate towards our dreams.

26

1987 Chevrolet Express Concept

In the captivating realm of automotive innovation, where dreams become reality, let's journey back to the year 1987 and explore the mesmerizing Chevrolet Express Concept. This remarkable creation wasn't just a car; it was a vision of the future, a bold declaration of Chevrolet's commitment to pushing the boundaries of design and technology.

Picture this: the late '80s, a time when utility vehicles were primarily defined by their practicality rather than their design. But Chevrolet, with its Express Concept, aimed to change that narrative. It was a concept ahead of its time, both in its aesthetics and technological advancements.

The Chevrolet Express Concept was a glimpse into a future where utility vehicles would be more than just tools; they would be works of art. Its design was a harmonious blend of sleek, aerodynamic lines, futuristic curves, and bold, angular features. It didn't just break the mold; it shattered it. This concept car challenged the status quo, showing that utility and style could coexist.

But the Express Concept wasn't just about looks; it was a technological marvel as well. In an era when onboard computers were still relatively new, this concept boasted advanced electronic systems that could monitor vehicle diagnostics, enhancing the driving experience and simplifying maintenance.

While the Express Concept didn't make it into mass production, its influence was profound. It ignited a spark in the automotive industry, inspiring the design of future utility vehicles. Concepts like this paved the way for the stylish, versatile SUVs and crossovers we see today, proving that practicality and aesthetics could go hand in hand.

So, when you look back at the 1987 Chevrolet Express Concept, don't just see a car; see a beacon of innovation. It's a reminder that the automotive world is a place of boundless creativity, where daring ideas can shape the future. This concept was Chevrolet's way of saying, "We're not just building cars; we're crafting dreams." And in doing so, it left an indelible mark on the road to automotive excellence.

27

1987 Nissan Saurus

Imagine a realm where creativity reigns and the road becomes a canvas for the boldest of artistic visions. In this landscape of automotive imagination, the Nissan Saurus emerges as a masterpiece that fuses design with innovation, a concept car that doesn't just challenge the norm but reinvents it.

Picture the mesmerizing era of the 1980s, a time when the world was captivated by possibilities and futuristic dreams. Amidst this tapestry of change, the Nissan Saurus takes its place – a concept car that dares to transform the mundane into the extraordinary. Conceived by the visionary minds at Nissan, this concept car embodies a philosophy of pushing boundaries and crafting a harmony of style and performance.

The Saurus's design is an embodiment of sleek lines and cutting-edge aesthetics, a symphony of form and function that captivates the eye. Its low, streamlined profile exudes an air of speed and modernity, while the bold angles and futuristic detailing hint at its avant-garde spirit. The vibrant blue hue, like an electric current, mirrors the car's essence of energy and innovation.

Yet, the Saurus's significance resonates far beyond its captivating exterior. Beneath its surface lies a realm of groundbreaking technology and engineering brilliance. This concept car showcased Nissan's prowess in aerodynamics and materials, introducing innovative ideas that would eventually influence the brand's production vehicles. Its turbocharged engine and lightweight construction exemplified performance and efficiency.

In 1987, the Nissan Saurus made its entrancing debut, captivating onlookers with its blend of form and function. Its influence, however, continued to resonate beyond its initial unveiling. The Saurus's design cues and technological experiments found their way into Nissan's future vehicles, shaping the brand's approach to design and engineering.

As you conjure the image of the Nissan Saurus, let it spark your own aspirations to blend innovation with aesthetics in your endeavors. Let it remind you that true greatness often involves embracing the uncharted and pushing limits. Just as the Saurus's groundbreaking design and innovative technologies influenced Nissan's journey, so too can your audacious spirit shape the trajectory of your dreams. Its legacy isn't confined to its striking design or technological marvels; it's a testament to the idea that the fusion of passion, engineering, and courage can shape industries and inspire us to accelerate towards our aspirations.

28

1990 Chevrolet Corvette CERV III

Welcome to a realm where innovation runs like a river and design is the language of dreams. In this world of automotive imagination, the Chevrolet Corvette CERV III emerges as a testament to the marriage of technology and artistry, a concept car that not only pushes the boundaries but rewrites the very script of high-performance driving.

Imagine a time when the horizon seemed limitless, a period marked by the pursuit of speed and the dance of engineering possibilities. In this era of boundless aspiration, the Chevrolet Corvette CERV III takes its place – a creation that dares to embody the future of performance in every line and curve. Brought to life by the ingenious minds at Chevrolet, this concept car encapsulates a philosophy of audacity and relentless engineering innovation.

The CERV III's design is an embodiment of aerodynamics and precision, a fusion of aesthetics and function that commands the wind's embrace. Its low-slung profile exudes an air of velocity and purpose, while the sculpted lines and bold detailing hint at its commitment to innovation. The gleaming metallic finish, like liquid silver, mirrors the car's essence of modernity and motion.

Yet, the CERV III's significance resonates far beyond its captivating exterior. Below its sculpted skin lies a world of revolutionary technology and engineering brilliance. This concept car embraced cutting-edge features like active suspension and advanced materials, showcasing Chevrolet's dedication to pioneering high-performance solutions. Its mid-engine layout heralded a new era of Corvette design, influencing the brand's trajectory.

1990 CHEVROLET CORVETTE CERV III

In 1990, the Chevrolet Corvette CERV III made its dazzling entrance, capturing attention with its blend of form and function. Its influence, however, extended beyond its initial unveiling. The CERV III's technological marvels and design cues found their way into Chevrolet's future vehicles, shaping the brand's approach to high-performance driving and engineering excellence.

As you envision the Chevrolet Corvette CERV III, let it awaken your own aspirations to blend technology with aesthetics in your pursuits. Let it remind you that true greatness often involves challenging conventions and embracing the cutting-edge. Just as the CERV III's groundbreaking design and innovative technologies influenced Chevrolet's journey, so too can your own audacious spirit shape the trajectory of your dreams. Its legacy isn't confined to its breathtaking design or pioneering technology; it's a testament to the idea that the fusion of passion, engineering, and courage can shape industries and inspire us to accelerate towards our aspirations.

29

1990 BMW Z18

Enter a realm where innovation meets artistry, where the road transforms into a canvas for groundbreaking design. In this world of automotive imagination, the BMW Z18 emerges as a testament to the marriage of aesthetics and engineering, a concept car that not only envisions the future but sets the stage for a new era of automotive elegance.

Imagine a time when design was more than just function—it was an expression of emotion, a statement of style. In this era of creative exploration, the BMW Z18 takes its place – a creation that doesn't just blur the lines between art and engineering, but transcends them. Crafted by the visionary minds at BMW, this concept car embodies a philosophy of pushing the boundaries of form and function.

The Z18's design is an embodiment of sleekness and sophistication, a symphony of curves and angles that captivate the eye and the wind alike. Its low-slung profile exudes an air of elegance and modernity, while the harmonious lines and intricate detailing hint at its German precision. The gleaming exterior finish, like a reflection of aspirations, mirrors the car's essence of luxury and innovation.

Yet, the Z18's significance extends beyond its captivating exterior. Underneath its sculpted exterior lies a realm of technological brilliance. This concept car introduced the world to BMW's commitment to innovative features, showcasing advanced technology and a focus on driving experience. Its balance of performance and design foreshadowed the direction of BMW's future vehicles.

In 1995, the BMW Z18 made its striking entrance, captivating enthusiasts with its blend of form and function. Its influence, however, resonated far beyond its initial unveiling. The Z18's blend of aesthetics and engineering innovation found their way into BMW's production vehicles, shaping the brand's approach to design and performance.

As you envision the BMW Z18, let it ignite your own aspirations to blend innovation with aesthetics in your pursuits. Let it remind you that true greatness often involves pushing the boundaries of creativity and embracing the extraordinary. Just as the Z18's pursuit of elegance and groundbreaking design influenced BMW's journey, so too can your audacious spirit shape the trajectory of your dreams. Its legacy isn't confined to its striking design or technological innovation; it's a testament to the idea that the fusion of passion, engineering, and courage can create masterpieces that inspire us to accelerate towards our aspirations.

30

1991 Mazda 787B Concept

Imagine a world where speed is a melody and innovation is the conductor of the symphony. In this realm of automotive creativity, the Mazda 787B Concept emerges as a masterpiece that merges engineering brilliance with the spirit of competition, a concept car that not only races against the wind but races against time itself.

Picture an era when tracks echoed with the roar of engines and hearts raced alongside tire treads. In this era of relentless pursuit, the Mazda 787B Concept takes center stage – a creation that doesn't just embrace the racetrack, but becomes one with it. Conceived by the ingenious minds at Mazda, this concept car embodies a philosophy of pushing the limits and crafting a fusion of performance and artistry.

The 787B Concept's design is an embodiment of aerodynamics and aggression, a symphony of lines that slices through the air with precision. Its low, sleek profile exudes an air of speed and purpose, while the bold angles and intricate detailing hint at its racing pedigree. The vibrant livery, like a streak of motion, captures the car's essence of competition and innovation.

Yet, the 787B Concept's significance stretches far beyond its captivating exterior. Underneath its dynamic shell lies a realm of groundbreaking technology and engineering brilliance. This concept car introduced the world to the power of Mazda's iconic rotary engine, showcasing the brand's commitment to pushing the boundaries of performance. Its pioneering engine technology and aerodynamic design laid the groundwork for Mazda's racing endeavors.

1991 MAZDA 787B CONCEPT

In 1991, the Mazda 787B Concept roared onto the stage, captivating racing enthusiasts with its blend of form and function. Its influence, however, reverberated beyond its initial unveiling. The 787B Concept's racing heritage and innovative technologies found their way into Mazda's future vehicles, shaping the brand's approach to performance and engineering.

As you imagine the Mazda 787B Concept, let it ignite your own aspirations to push boundaries and merge innovation with artistry in your pursuits. Let it remind you that true greatness often involves embracing the unknown and accelerating towards challenges. Just as the 787B Concept's groundbreaking technologies and racing spirit influenced Mazda's trajectory, so too can your own audacious spirit shape the course of your dreams. Its legacy isn't confined to its breathtaking design or pioneering technology; it's a testament to the idea that the fusion of passion, engineering, and courage can shape industries and inspire us to accelerate towards our aspirations.

31

1992 Ford Ghia Focus Concept

Imagine a world where innovation and style intertwine, where the road becomes a runway for futuristic designs. In this realm of automotive artistry, the Ford Ghia Focus Concept emerges as a beacon of elegance and technological prowess, a concept car that doesn't merely predict the future, but crafts it with meticulous attention to detail.

1992 FORD GHIA FOCUS CONCEPT

Picture a time when automotive design was more than functionality; it was an embodiment of dreams and aspirations. In this era of visionary exploration, the Ford Ghia Focus Concept takes center stage – a creation that seamlessly blends aesthetics and technology. Conceived as a collaboration between Ford and Ghia, this concept car embodies a philosophy of pushing design boundaries and sculpting the future of mobility.

The Ghia Focus Concept's design is an embodiment of grace and modernity, a symphony of sleek lines that capture both the eye's attention and the wind's embrace. Its refined profile exudes an air of sophistication and contemporary flair, while the bold contours and intricate detailing hint at its innovative spirit. The luminous exterior finish, like a radiant vision, mirrors the car's essence of elegance and advanced design.

Yet, the Ghia Focus Concept's significance spans beyond its captivating exterior. Beneath its sleek surface lies a world of revolutionary technology and engineering brilliance. This concept car introduced advanced features like touchscreen interfaces and futuristic interior elements, showcasing Ford's dedication to blending cutting-edge technology with timeless design.

In 1992, the Ford Ghia Focus Concept made its entrancing debut, captivating enthusiasts with its blend of form and function. Its influence, however, reached beyond its initial unveiling. The Ghia Focus Concept's forward-thinking design and innovative technologies found their way into Ford's future vehicles, shaping the brand's approach to modernizing interiors and incorporating advanced technology.

As you conjure the image of the Ford Ghia Focus Concept, let it spark your own aspirations to blend aesthetics with technology in your pursuits. Let it remind you that true greatness often involves embracing innovation and crafting a future that merges sophistication with functionality. Just as the Ghia Focus Concept's visionary design and pioneering technologies influenced Ford's journey, so too can your audacious spirit shape the trajectory of your dreams. Its legacy isn't confined to its striking design or advanced technology; it's a testament to the idea that the fusion of passion, engineering, and courage can shape industries and inspire us to accelerate towards our aspirations.

32

1993 Aston Martin DB7 V12 Prototype TWR

Step into a world where elegance meets exhilaration, where the dance of design and engineering creates a masterpiece on wheels. In this realm of automotive artistry, the Aston Martin DB7 V12 Prototype TWR emerges as a fusion of sophistication and power, a concept car that doesn't just redefine luxury but embodies a philosophy of crafting excellence from every angle.

Imagine a time when the road beckoned with promise, a period marked by the pursuit of speed and the quest for refinement. In this era of visionary exploration, the Aston Martin DB7 V12 Prototype TWR takes center stage – a creation that goes beyond convention to redefine the very essence of grand touring. Conceived through the collaborative brilliance of Aston Martin and Tom Walkinshaw Racing (TWR), this concept car encapsulates a philosophy of blending performance and luxury into a harmonious symphony.

The DB7 V12 Prototype TWR's design is an embodiment of graceful lines and muscular presence, a marriage of aesthetics and power that captivates the eye. Its low, curvaceous profile exudes an air of grace and velocity, while the timeless lines and refined detailing hint at its British heritage. The lustrous metallic finish, like a mirror reflecting aspiration, mirrors the car's essence of prestige and performance.

Yet, the Prototype TWR's significance reaches far beyond its captivating exterior. Under its skin lies a realm of pioneering technology and engineering brilliance. This concept car introduced a mighty V12 engine and advanced performance features, showcasing Aston Martin and TWR's dedication to crafting a dynamic driving experience. Its blend of power and luxury laid the foundation for future Aston Martin vehicles, influencing the brand's trajectory.

In 1993, the Aston Martin DB7 V12 Prototype TWR made its entrancing debut, captivating enthusiasts with its blend of form and force. Its influence, however, extended beyond its initial unveiling. The Prototype TWR's dynamic performance and blend of refinement found their way into Aston Martin's production cars, shaping the brand's future and its approach to creating vehicles that embrace both speed and luxury.

As you envision the Aston Martin DB7 V12 Prototype TWR, let it kindle your own aspirations to marry elegance with power in your pursuits. Let it remind you that true greatness often involves challenging the boundaries and embracing the extraordinary. Just as the Prototype TWR's pursuit of performance and seamless luxury influenced Aston Martin's journey, so too can your own audacious spirit shape the course of your dreams. Its legacy isn't confined to its striking design or pioneering technology; it's a testament to the idea that the fusion of passion, engineering, and courage can create masterpieces that inspire us to accelerate towards our aspirations.

33

1993 Mercedes-Benz Vision A93

Step into a world where dreams meet the road, where imagination fuels innovation and the future of mobility takes shape. In this realm of automotive exploration, the Mercedes-Benz Vision A93 emerges as a visionary masterpiece, a concept car that doesn't just glimpse tomorrow's possibilities but paves the way for a new era of design and technology.

Imagine a time when innovation danced on the horizon, an era marked by the pursuit of sustainable luxury and cutting-edge advancements. In this era of forward thinking, the Mercedes-Benz Vision A93 takes center stage – a creation that embodies the essence of Mercedes-Benz's commitment to shaping the future of transportation. Born from the visionary minds at Mercedes-Benz, this concept car encapsulates a philosophy of embracing sustainability and redefining driving experience.

The Vision A93's design is an embodiment of sleekness and sophistication, a symphony of form and function that captures the eye's attention and the wind's embrace. Its contemporary profile exudes an air of modernity and grace, while the fluid lines and innovative detailing hint at its commitment to reshaping the conventional. The ethereal hues, like hues of progress, mirror the car's essence of elegance and innovation.

Yet, the Vision A93's significance spans far beyond its captivating exterior. Beneath its surface lies a world of revolutionary technology and engineering brilliance. This concept car showcases Mercedes-Benz's dedication to sustainability and innovation, featuring advanced electric propulsion and cutting-edge interior connectivity. Its approach to eco-conscious luxury and intelligent design influenced Mercedes-Benz's vision for the vehicles of tomorrow.

1993 MERCEDES-BENZ VISION A93

In 1993, the Mercedes-Benz Vision A93 made its entrancing debut, captivating imaginations with its blend of form and function. Its influence, however, extended beyond its initial unveiling. The Vision A93's focus on sustainability and forward-thinking design elements found their way into Mercedes-Benz's future production vehicles, shaping the brand's approach to luxury and performance.

As you conjure the image of the Mercedes-Benz Vision A93, let it ignite your own aspirations to blend innovation with sustainability in your pursuits. Let it remind you that true greatness often involves embracing change and paving the way for a brighter future. Just as the Vision A93's revolutionary technologies and visionary design influenced Mercedes-Benz's trajectory, so too can your audacious spirit shape the course of your dreams. Its legacy isn't confined to its breathtaking design or pioneering technology; it's a testament to the idea that the fusion of passion, engineering, and courage can shape industries and inspire us to accelerate towards our aspirations.

34

1995 Ford GT90

Imagine a machine so spectacular, so extraordinary, that it seems like it was plucked straight from the dreams of a visionary. Meet the Ford GT90, a concept car that not only pushed the boundaries of automotive engineering but also left an indelible mark on the world of supercars.

The Ford GT90 made its debut in 1995, and it was a beacon of futuristic design and groundbreaking technology. This automotive masterpiece was Ford's way of paying homage to the legendary GT40, a car that had achieved iconic status by winning the 24 Hours of Le Mans four times in a row during the 1960s.

At first glance, the GT90 appeared to be a creation from the distant future. Its angular, aerodynamic body was a symphony of sharp lines and aggressive curves, hinting at the sheer power that resided beneath its hood. The design was not just about aesthetics; it was a result of extensive wind tunnel testing to ensure optimal aerodynamic performance.

But what truly set the GT90 apart was its heart—a quad-turbocharged V12 engine. With a staggering 720 horsepower, it could sprint from 0 to 60 mph in just 3.1 seconds, a mind-blowing feat in the mid-1990s. This raw power was harnessed through a six-speed manual gearbox, adding to the car's allure for driving enthusiasts.

In terms of innovation, the GT90 was a marvel. It featured a carbon-fiber monocoque chassis, a technology rarely seen in production cars at the time. The body was constructed from lightweight materials like carbon fiber and aluminum to keep its weight in check. Inside, the cabin was a blend of luxury and technology, with features like a digital instrument cluster and a central control screen that were ahead of their time.

While the Ford GT90 never made it to the production line, it served as a technological showcase and a source of inspiration for future Ford performance cars. Elements of its design, such as the use of lightweight materials and aerodynamic efficiency, influenced the development of the Ford GT, a production supercar that became a symbol of Ford's commitment to performance.

In the world of concept cars, the Ford GT90 is a legend. It represents the audacious spirit of automotive innovation, where engineers and designers dared to dream beyond the confines of convention. Even though it never graced our driveways, its legacy lives on in the hearts of automotive enthusiasts and as a testament to the limitless possibilities of automotive design and engineering.

35

1995 Toyota MRJ Concept

Ladies and gentlemen, prepare to step into the future of automotive innovation with the 1995 Toyota MRJ Concept. Picture this: the mid-'90s, a time when the automotive world was on the brink of a technological revolution, and Toyota decided to set the stage with a concept that would rewrite the rules of the road.

The MRJ, which stands for "Midship Runabout Joy," was unveiled in 1995, and it was a true marvel of its time. It was not just a car; it was a manifesto of Toyota's unwavering commitment to pushing the boundaries of design and engineering.

At first glance, the MRJ is a vision of aerodynamic excellence. Its low-slung body, flowing lines, and distinctive gull-wing doors made it an instant head-turner. The design philosophy behind the MRJ was to create a car that looked like it was in constant motion, even when standing still, a testament to the harmony between form and function.

But the MRJ Concept was more than just a pretty face. Under the hood, it showcased innovative technologies that were far ahead of its time. This concept car was equipped with a mid-mounted engine, a layout typically reserved for high-performance sports cars. It provided exceptional balance and handling, turning every twist and turn of the road into a thrilling experience.

Inside, the MRJ was a blend of luxury and futurism. Its cockpit was designed with the driver in mind, placing all controls within easy reach. Technological features included a sophisticated infotainment system and digital instrumentation, a sign of the digital age that was dawning.

The influence of the 1995 Toyota MRJ Concept reverberated through the automotive industry. While it may not have been mass-produced itself, its design elements and mid-engine layout inspired future Toyota models, including the beloved Toyota MR2 and even the iconic Toyota 86.

But the MRJ's impact goes beyond Toyota. It reminded the entire industry of the importance of pushing boundaries, of daring to dream and create concepts that not only show what's possible but also influence the vehicles that we drive every day.

In essence, the 1995 Toyota MRJ Concept was a beacon of inspiration. It challenged conventional thinking and set the stage for a new era of automotive innovation, where design, technology, and performance could come together to create something truly extraordinary. It showed us that, in the world of automobiles, the future is limited only by our imagination.

36

1996 Mercedes-Benz F200

In the swirling tapestry of automotive history, the Mercedes-Benz F200 concept car stands as a beacon of innovation, a testament to the boundless spirit of engineering that defines the brand. Transport yourself to the year 1996, where the F200 made its grand entrance onto the global stage, showcasing a vision of the future that would influence the cars we drive today.

Imagine a world where your car is not just a machine, but a partner attuned to your every need. The F200 was designed to create this very synergy between man and machine, blurring the lines between driving and being driven. At its core was a philosophy that cars should adapt to the driver, not the other way around.

One of the most captivating aspects of the F200 was its novel "Drive-by-Wire" technology, a concept that would later become a staple in modern vehicles. It allowed the car to respond instantly to the driver's inputs, without the need for traditional mechanical linkages. This was a pivotal step towards the autonomous driving systems we see today.

Now, let's dive into its design. The F200 was an avant-garde masterpiece, a rolling sculpture that pushed the boundaries of what was considered possible in automotive aesthetics. Its gullwing doors, reminiscent of the iconic 300SL, gave it a futuristic edge, while the absence of a B-pillar created an inviting and open cabin space.

Step inside, and you'd be greeted by an interior that felt like it was plucked from the pages of a science fiction novel. A swiveling passenger seat allowed for face-to-face interaction, fostering a sense of community within the car. The driver's seat, equipped with an intuitive joystick control, evoked the feel of a pilot's cockpit, emphasizing the car's connection to aeronautics.

The F200's influence on mass production cars can be seen in various aspects of today's vehicles. Drive-by-Wire technology, once a concept, is now a reality in many modern cars, enhancing safety and performance. The focus on adaptable interiors and the blending of luxury with cutting-edge technology has become a hallmark of the Mercedes-Benz brand.

In essence, the F200 was more than just a concept car; it was a harbinger of an automotive future where vehicles seamlessly integrated with our lives. It dared to ask, "What if?" and, in doing so, redefined the way we think about cars. So, when you see a sleek, tech-laden luxury car on the road today, remember that the Mercedes-Benz F200 played a part in shaping that future. It was a glimpse into tomorrow's world, and its influence still echoes in the cars we drive today.

37

1999 Cadillac Evoq

Imagine a world where luxury and innovation fuse seamlessly, where the road becomes a canvas for a masterpiece of design and technology. In this realm of automotive imagination, the Cadillac Evoq emerges as a symbol of elegance and futuristic vision, a concept car that doesn't just predict the future, but breathes life into it with bold creativity.

Picture a time when automotive dreams were sculpted by the finest minds in design and engineering. In this era of boundless possibilities, the Cadillac Evoq takes center stage – a creation that doesn't merely reimagine luxury, but reshapes it. Brought to life by the visionary minds at Cadillac, this concept car embodies a philosophy of embracing cutting-edge technology while paying homage to timeless sophistication.

The Evoq's design is an embodiment of fluid lines and opulence, a symphony of curves that captivate the senses and the wind alike. Its low-slung profile exudes an air of grandeur and modernity, while the graceful detailing and bold accents hint at its American heritage. The lustrous finish, like liquid luxury, mirrors the car's essence of opulence and innovation.

Yet, the Evoq's significance reaches far beyond its captivating exterior. Beneath its surface lies a world of revolutionary technology and engineering brilliance. This concept car introduced features like Night Vision and Magnetic Ride Control, showcasing Cadillac's commitment to pushing the boundaries of luxury and performance. Its blend of cutting-edge tech and design elements influenced Cadillac's trajectory towards modernization.

In 1999, the Cadillac Evoq made its entrancing debut, capturing imaginations with its blend of form and function. Its influence, however, extended beyond its initial unveiling. The Evoq's futuristic design and innovative technologies found their way into Cadillac's production vehicles, shaping the brand's approach to modern luxury and incorporating advanced features.

As you conjure the image of the Cadillac Evoq, let it spark your own aspirations to blend opulence with innovation in your pursuits. Let it remind you that true greatness often involves embracing the possibilities of technology while honoring the roots of timeless elegance. Just as the Evoq's forward-thinking design and pioneering technologies influenced Cadillac's journey, so too can your audacious spirit shape the course of your dreams. Its legacy isn't confined to its breathtaking design or groundbreaking technology; it's a testament to the idea that the fusion of passion, engineering, and courage can shape industries and inspire us to accelerate towards our aspirations.

38

1999 Bugatti Veyron Concept

Ladies and gentlemen, step into the world of automotive legend with the Bugatti Veyron Concept, a car that redefined the limits of speed, luxury, and engineering excellence. Imagine a vehicle that effortlessly combines the elegance of a supercar with the raw power of a fighter jet.

The Bugatti Veyron Concept was first unveiled in 1999, and it was a vision of automotive excellence from the very start. It was the brainchild of the Volkswagen Group, which had acquired Bugatti in the late 1990s. The concept was named after the racing driver Pierre Veyron, who won the 24 Hours of Le Mans for Bugatti in 1939.

What sets the Veyron Concept apart is its relentless pursuit of speed. It was designed to break records and shatter expectations. The heart of this beast was an 8.0-liter quad-turbocharged W16 engine, a powerplant that was nothing short of a marvel. It unleashed a mind-boggling 1,001 horsepower, propelling the car from 0 to 60 miles per hour in less than 2.5 seconds.

But it wasn't just about brute force; the Veyron Concept was a symphony of aerodynamics and precision engineering. Its sleek, low-slung design wasn't just for show; it was carefully sculpted to reduce drag and provide the necessary downforce to keep this speed demon glued to the tarmac. The streamlined body, the signature Bugatti grille, and the distinctive C-shaped side profile all contributed to its breathtaking appearance.

One of the most remarkable features of the Veyron Concept was its top speed. It could reach an astonishing 253 miles per hour, making it the fastest production car in the world at the time. To achieve this, Bugatti had to develop tires that could withstand such incredible forces and engineering solutions to keep the car stable even at blistering speeds.

In 2005, the Bugatti Veyron 16.4, based on the original concept, became a reality and entered production. It continued to break records, cementing its status as an engineering marvel. It showcased the cutting-edge technology that could be applied to mass production cars, pushing the boundaries of what was considered possible in the automotive industry.

The Veyron's influence on the automotive world was profound. It sparked a horsepower war among supercar manufacturers, pushing them to develop ever more powerful and faster cars. The lessons learned from the Veyron's development, from aerodynamics to tire technology, have trickled down into more accessible sports cars, making them faster and more capable.

In essence, the Bugatti Veyron Concept is a symbol of human achievement. It represents the relentless pursuit of perfection, the desire to push the limits of what's possible, and the marriage of art and engineering in the form of a four-wheeled masterpiece. It's a reminder that in the world of automotive design and technology, there are no limits, only new horizons to conquer.

39

2000 Audi Rosemeyer

Imagine a world where the winds whisper secrets of speed and design, where the road becomes a theater for innovation and elegance. In this realm of automotive dreams, the Audi Rosemeyer emerges as a symphony of power and grace, a concept car that doesn't just push the boundaries, but redefines them with audacious creativity.

2000 AUDI ROSEMEYER

Picture an era when the pursuit of speed was an art form, and technology danced in harmony with aesthetics. In this era of visionary exploration, the Audi Rosemeyer takes center stage – a creation that doesn't merely embrace tradition but transcends it. Crafted by the visionary minds at Audi, this concept car encapsulates a philosophy of pushing engineering limits while celebrating the spirit of racing heritage.

The Rosemeyer's design is an embodiment of sleek lines and aerodynamic elegance, a fusion of form and function that captures both the eye's attention and the wind's embrace. Its low, sweeping profile exudes an air of velocity and modernity, while the bold contours and iconic grille hint at its racing inspiration. The metallic finish, like a reflection of dreams, mirrors the car's essence of speed and innovation.

Yet, the Rosemeyer's significance spans far beyond its captivating exterior. Beneath its sculpted surface lies a realm of groundbreaking technology and engineering brilliance. This concept car showcased Audi's commitment to performance, featuring a powerful engine and advanced aerodynamics. Its innovative approach to materials and design laid the foundation for Audi's future racing endeavors.

In 2000, the Audi Rosemeyer made its electrifying entrance, captivating enthusiasts with its blend of form and function. Its influence, however, stretched beyond its initial unveiling. The Rosemeyer's racing DNA and innovative technologies found their way into Audi's future production vehicles, shaping the brand's approach to performance and incorporating high-performance elements.

As you imagine the Audi Rosemeyer, let it spark your own aspirations to blend power with elegance in your pursuits. Let it remind you that true greatness often involves embracing innovation while respecting heritage. Just as the Rosemeyer's pursuit of speed and groundbreaking technology influenced Audi's journey, so too can your audacious spirit shape the trajectory of your dreams. Its legacy isn't confined to its stunning design or pioneering technology; it's a testament to the idea that the fusion of passion, engineering, and courage can create masterpieces that inspire us to accelerate towards our aspirations.

40

2001 Chrysler Crossfire

Imagine a world where the fusion of beauty and power takes the shape of a work of art on wheels, where innovation is sculpted into every curve. In this realm of automotive elegance, the Chrysler Crossfire emerges as a symphony of design and engineering, a concept car that not only redefines aesthetics but sets the stage for a new era of automotive excellence.

Picture an era when the road became a runway for bold ideas, and craftsmanship was elevated to an art form. In this era of creative exploration, the Chrysler Crossfire takes its place – a creation that doesn't just redefine beauty, but shapes the very essence of contemporary design. Brought to life by the visionary minds at Chrysler, this concept car embodies a philosophy of blending sophistication with performance.

The Crossfire's design is an embodiment of sleek lines and dynamic presence, a marriage of form and function that captures both the eye's attention and the wind's embrace. Its low-slung profile exudes an air of elegance and modernity, while the sweeping curves and bold creases hint at its German-American heritage. The gleaming finish, like a reflection of dreams, mirrors the car's essence of style and innovation.

Yet, the Crossfire's significance reaches far beyond its captivating exterior. Beneath its sculpted surface lies a realm of innovative technology and engineering brilliance. This concept car introduced advanced aerodynamics and performance features, showcasing Chrysler's dedication to pushing the boundaries of design and driving experience. Its blend of artistry and performance served as a harbinger of the brand's future direction.

2001 CHRYSLER CROSSFIRE

In 2001, the Chrysler Crossfire made its breathtaking entrance, captivating enthusiasts with its blend of form and function. Its influence, however, resonated beyond its initial unveiling. The Crossfire's bold design and innovative technologies found their way into Chrysler's production vehicles, shaping the brand's approach to blending aesthetics with performance.

As you conjure the image of the Chrysler Crossfire, let it spark your own aspirations to blend style with substance in your pursuits. Let it remind you that true greatness often involves marrying aesthetics with engineering, crafting a future where beauty and innovation coexist. Just as the Crossfire's design prowess and performance influence shaped Chrysler's journey, so too can your audacious spirit shape the trajectory of your dreams. Its legacy isn't confined to its striking design or innovative features; it's a testament to the idea that the fusion of passion, engineering, and courage can shape industries and inspire us to accelerate towards our aspirations.

41

2001 Nissan GT-R Concept

In the world of high-performance sports cars, one name stands out as a symbol of raw power, innovation, and relentless pursuit of excellence - the Nissan GT-R Concept.

Picture yourself standing in the presence of automotive greatness. The year is 2001, and Nissan has just unveiled the GT-R Concept, teasing the world with a glimpse into the future of sports car design and engineering.

From the very first glance, you can tell that this is not an ordinary car. Its body is a masterpiece of aerodynamics, sculpted to slice through the air like a bullet. The GT-R Concept's signature feature, the quad-circle taillights, adds a futuristic touch to its otherwise aggressive stance. This design, although avant-garde at the time, has since become an iconic symbol of the GT-R lineage.

Step inside, and you're greeted by a cockpit that feels like it belongs in a fighter jet. The driver-centric layout, with a multifunctional display and an array of buttons and knobs, shows Nissan's dedication to providing the ultimate driving experience. This is not just a car; it's a machine engineered to make you feel like a race car driver every time you slide behind the wheel.

But it's under the hood where the GT-R Concept truly shines. The heart of this beast is a twin-turbocharged V6 engine, a technological marvel that produces a staggering amount of power. It's a testament to Nissan's commitment to pushing the boundaries of what's possible in a production car. The GT-R Concept's engine technology paved the way for the production version, the Nissan GT-R, which became known as the "Godzilla" of sports cars.

Released in 2007, the Nissan GT-R took the automotive world by storm. Its advanced all-wheel-drive system, lightning-fast dual-clutch transmission, and powerful engine made it a dominant force on both the road and the track. The GT-R's performance capabilities were a direct result of the innovative technologies first showcased in the GT-R Concept.

This iconic concept car not only influenced the mass production of the Nissan GT-R but also inspired a new era of sports car design and engineering. It proved that cutting-edge technology and heart-pounding performance could coexist in a single machine, setting a standard that many other manufacturers have since aspired to.

So, whenever you see a Nissan GT-R prowling the streets, remember that it all began with a visionary concept - a concept that dared to redefine the boundaries of automotive performance and style. The Nissan GT-R Concept remains an enduring symbol of what's possible when imagination meets engineering prowess, a reminder that the pursuit of perfection is a journey without limits.

42

2001 Honda NSX-R Concept

Step into the world of automotive legends with the Honda NSX-R Concept, a car that combines the essence of racing performance with the innovation of Japanese engineering. This iconic concept car, which emerged from the dreams of Honda's designers and engineers, set the stage for a new era of sports cars, both in design and technological prowess.

Imagine a crisp morning in 2001, where automotive enthusiasts and industry experts alike gathered to witness the unveiling of a concept that would leave an indelible mark. As the curtains fell, the Honda NSX-R Concept revealed itself, embodying the spirit of racing in every line and curve.

The NSX-R Concept's design was a masterpiece of aerodynamics and aggression, a reflection of its racing pedigree. Its low, sleek profile, sharp angles, and bold red accents conveyed a sense of purpose - the purpose to dominate both on the track and on the road.

However, it was under the hood where the NSX-R Concept truly shone. This was not merely a sports car; it was an embodiment of Honda's commitment to performance and innovation. Nestled within the car's lightweight chassis was a high-revving V6 engine, carefully engineered to deliver exhilarating speed and power. The engine's placement in the middle of the car ensured optimal weight distribution, resulting in exceptional handling and cornering capabilities.

But what truly set the NSX-R Concept apart was its innovative use of materials and technologies. Honda had employed advanced lightweight materials, including aluminum and carbon fiber, to keep the car's weight to a minimum. This not only enhanced performance but also improved fuel efficiency.

The NSX-R Concept's influence on mass production cars was profound. It was a harbinger of Honda's commitment to precision engineering and innovation, which would go on to shape future models. Elements of its design, such as the aerodynamic sculpting and mid-engine layout, found their way into subsequent Honda sports cars.

2001 HONDA NSX-R CONCEPT

Moreover, the NSX-R Concept symbolized a resurgence of Japanese sports car dominance in the early 2000s, reminding the world of Japan's engineering prowess. It inspired a new generation of sports cars that combined cutting-edge technology with thrilling performance.

In the automotive world, the Honda NSX-R Concept remains a symbol of passion, precision, and performance. It serves as a reminder that dreams, when combined with innovation and a dedication to excellence, can create machines that not only redefine the limits of speed but also leave an enduring legacy in the world of sports cars.

43

2002 Lexus 2054

Step into the realm of imagination and envision a world where cars aren't just modes of transportation; they're works of art and vessels of innovation.

In this world, there's a car that captured hearts and minds, the Lexus 2054.

Though we still haven't reached the year 2054, this concept car made its unforgettable debut in the blockbuster movie "Minority Report" in 2002, directed by Steven Spielberg. It was a glimpse into the distant future, an era where cars had evolved beyond our wildest dreams.

The Lexus 2054 is not your average car; it's a masterpiece of futuristic design and technological marvels. Its striking, aerodynamic form resembles a silver bullet, an embodiment of speed and precision. The wheels, devoid of traditional spokes, seemed to float beneath the sleek body, defying gravity.

But what truly set the Lexus 2054 apart were the innovative technologies it showcased. In the film, it was depicted as a self-driving, autonomous vehicle, a concept that was, at the time, still in its infancy. The car seamlessly glided through cityscapes, navigating with precision and reacting to its surroundings in real-time. It was a vision of a future where accidents were nearly unheard of, and commuting was a stress-free experience.

The Lexus 2054, although a concept born on the silver screen, had a profound influence on the automotive industry. It inspired carmakers to push the boundaries of design and technology. Concepts once considered pure science fiction, like autonomous driving, are now becoming a reality.

So, as we journey towards the year 2054, let us remember the Lexus 2054 as a symbol of human innovation and the limitless possibilities of the future. It reminds us that, in the world of automobiles, the line between imagination and reality is beautifully blurred, and the cars of tomorrow are limited only by the bounds of our creativity.

44

2003 Ford GT40

Imagine a world where the spirit of racing meets the grace of design, where the road becomes a canvas for a symphony of power and beauty. In this realm of automotive artistry, the 2003 Ford GT40 emerges as a true testament to the legacy of speed and innovation, a concept car that doesn't just pay homage to history, but revitalizes it with a modern roar.

Picture an era when racing legends carved their stories into the tracks, where engineering brilliance was the key to victory. In this era of motorsport mystique, the 2003 Ford GT40 takes its place – a creation that doesn't merely revive a legacy, but propels it into the future. Brought to life by the visionary minds at Ford, this concept car embodies a philosophy of honoring heritage while embracing the cutting edge.

The GT40's design is an embodiment of aggression and aerodynamic prowess, a fusion of form and function that commands attention and the wind's embrace. Its sleek, low-slung profile exudes an air of speed and modernity, while the sweeping curves and iconic racing stripes hint at its legendary lineage. The vibrant finish, like a canvas of aspiration, mirrors the car's essence of performance and innovation.

Yet, the GT40's significance stretches far beyond its captivating exterior. Beneath its sculpted surface lies a world of advanced technology and engineering excellence. This concept car showcased Ford's commitment to pushing performance boundaries, featuring a powerful engine and cutting-edge aerodynamics. Its blend of racing heritage and modern design set the tone for Ford's future endeavors in the realm of high-performance vehicles.

2003 FORD GT40

In 2003, the Ford GT40 made its triumphant return, captivating enthusiasts with its blend of form and function. Its influence, however, reached beyond its initial unveiling. The GT40's racing DNA and performance excellence found their way into Ford's production vehicles, shaping the brand's approach to crafting supercars that redefine speed and aesthetics.

As you conjure the image of the 2003 Ford GT40, let it ignite your own aspirations to blend history with innovation in your pursuits. Let it remind you that true greatness often involves paying homage to the past while pushing the boundaries of the present. Just as the GT40's pursuit of speed and design excellence influenced Ford's journey, so too can your audacious spirit shape the trajectory of your dreams. Its legacy isn't confined to its striking design or racing lineage; it's a testament to the idea that the fusion of passion, engineering, and courage can shape industries and inspire us to accelerate towards our aspirations.

45

2003 Cadillac Sixteen

Imagine a world where luxury knows no bounds, where power and elegance collide in a symphony of automotive excellence. In the early 21st century, the

Cadillac Sixteen emerged as an embodiment of this vision, an iconic concept car that pushed the limits of opulence and innovation.

The year was 2003 when Cadillac unveiled the Sixteen Concept, a masterpiece that redefined the very essence of American luxury. As its name suggests, at its heart lay a colossal 13.6-liter V16 engine, a homage to Cadillac's historic 16-cylinder engines of the past. This monstrous powerplant churned out a breathtaking 1,000 horsepower, an awe-inspiring feat even by today's standards.

But the Sixteen wasn't just about sheer power; it was a manifestation of Cadillac's unwavering commitment to design excellence. Its exterior was a statement of sophistication, blending classic Cadillac elements with modern grace. The long, sweeping lines and the iconic wreath and crest emblem on the massive grille exuded a timeless sense of grandeur.

Step inside the cabin, and you'd find an oasis of luxury. The interior was adorned with sumptuous leather, exotic wood accents, and a waterfall console. It was a haven of comfort, equipped with cutting-edge technology that ensured an unparalleled driving experience.

Now, here's where the Cadillac Sixteen becomes truly iconic. It was more than just a concept; it was a philosophy. A bold declaration that American automakers could create vehicles that rivaled the best the world had to offer. While the Sixteen didn't make it into mass production, its influence was profound.

It served as a beacon of inspiration for Cadillac's future lineup, injecting elements of its design and technology into subsequent models. The Sixteen Concept pushed the boundaries of what was possible in the automotive world, setting new standards for luxury and performance.

In the end, the Cadillac Sixteen wasn't just a car; it was a symbol of ambition, a testament to the relentless pursuit of excellence. It showed that, in the world of automobiles, dreams could become reality, and the pursuit of perfection was a journey without end. So, when you think of the Sixteen, remember that it wasn't just a concept car; it was a vision of what's possible when innovation and luxury merge seamlessly.

46

2003 Mercedes F 500 Mind

In the world of concept cars, where imagination knows no bounds, there emerged a masterpiece that not only pushed the boundaries of design and technology but also ignited our dreams of the future. Ladies and gentlemen, meet the 2003 Mercedes F 500 Mind.

The very name "F 500 Mind" suggests a car that dares to venture into the realms of thought and consciousness, and indeed, this concept car did just that. Mercedes-Benz unveiled this visionary marvel in 2003, and it was a testament to the brand's relentless pursuit of innovation.

One of the most striking features of the F 500 Mind was its novel "Revolutionary Roof" system. This innovative roof could become transparent at the touch of a button, flooding the cabin with natural light or providing privacy and shade as desired. It was as if the car could adapt to your mood, making it a rolling sanctuary of comfort and serenity.

But the real magic happened inside. Step into the F 500 Mind, and you'd be greeted by a cabin bathed in futuristic luxury. The seats, equipped with "body scan" technology, would adjust their contours to fit your body perfectly, ensuring an unparalleled level of comfort during your journey. Imagine a car that intuitively knows how to pamper you.

The car also featured a novel "steer-by-wire" system, hinting at the future of autonomous driving. Instead of traditional mechanical links between the steering wheel and the wheels, the F 500 Mind used electronic signals to translate your intentions into precise movements, offering a glimpse of what driving could become.

Moreover, this concept car showcased Mercedes-Benz's commitment to sustainability with its advanced hybrid powertrain. It was a nod to a greener, more eco-conscious automotive future, a theme that would later become increasingly prominent in the industry.

The influence of the Mercedes F 500 Mind reverberated through the years, shaping the direction of luxury cars. Its ideas about adaptable, intuitive interiors, advanced driving technologies, and environmentally friendly power sources inspired the development of subsequent Mercedes-Benz models and even influenced the broader automotive industry.

As you contemplate this remarkable concept car, remember that it was not merely a car; it was a canvas upon which the future of automotive innovation was painted. The Mercedes F 500 Mind dared us to think beyond the confines of the present, to envision a world where our cars understand and adapt to our desires—a world where luxury and sustainability coexist harmoniously.

47

2004 Peugeot 907

Step into a world where elegance and performance intertwine, where the road becomes a runway for automotive dreams. In this realm of innovation, the Peugeot 907 emerges as a symphony of artistry and power, a concept car that doesn't just push boundaries, but redefines them with a touch of

2004 PEUGEOT 907

French sophistication.

Imagine an era when automotive design was a canvas for limitless imagination, and engineering prowess was a path to automotive excellence. In this era of creative exploration, the Peugeot 907 takes its place – a creation that doesn't merely embody beauty, but encapsulates the very essence of French design ingenuity. Crafted by the visionary minds at Peugeot, this concept car embodies a philosophy of marrying art with engineering.

The 907's design is an embodiment of grace and aerodynamic allure, a fusion of form and function that captivates both the eye and the wind's embrace. Its sweeping lines and sculpted curves exude an air of elegance and modernity, while the bold grille and distinctive logo hint at its French heritage. The shimmering finish, like a work of art, mirrors the car's essence of style and innovation.

Yet, the 907's significance transcends its captivating exterior. Beneath its surface lies a realm of cutting-edge technology and engineering brilliance. This concept car showcased Peugeot's commitment to pushing design boundaries, featuring advanced materials and aerodynamics. Its blend of elegance and performance paved the way for Peugeot's future endeavors in the realm of luxury and high-performance vehicles.

In 2004, the Peugeot 907 graced the world's stage, captivating enthusiasts with its blend of form and function. Its influence, however, echoed far beyond its initial unveiling. The 907's design philosophy and innovative approach to materials found their way into Peugeot's production vehicles, shaping the brand's approach to crafting vehicles that merge aesthetics with performance.

As you envision the Peugeot 907, let it ignite your own aspirations to blend artistry with engineering in your pursuits. Let it remind you that true greatness often involves pushing the boundaries of design while embracing the spirit of innovation. Just as the 907's pursuit of elegance and groundbreaking design influenced Peugeot's journey, so too can your audacious spirit shape the trajectory of your dreams. Its legacy isn't confined to its striking design or innovative features; it's a testament to the idea that the fusion of passion, engineering, and courage can create masterpieces that inspire us to accelerate towards our aspirations.

48

2005 Lexus LF-A Concept

Imagine a world where speed and elegance fuse into a symphony of automotive artistry, where the road itself becomes a canvas for the expression of performance and innovation. In this realm of automotive dreams, the 2005 Lexus LF-A Concept emerges as a testament to human ingenuity and a vision of a future where boundaries are redefined.

Think of an era when the pursuit of excellence wasn't limited to practicality, but was a bold exploration of what's possible. In this era of daring imagination, the 2005 Lexus LF-A Concept takes its place – not just as a car, but as a living embodiment of Lexus's pursuit of perfection. Brought to life by the visionary minds at Lexus, this concept car represents a fusion of passion and precision.

The LF-A Concept's design is a symphony of sculpted curves and bold lines, a blend of aesthetics and aerodynamics that not only captures attention but also dances with the wind. Its low, aggressive stance radiates a sense of power and modernity, while the distinctive Lexus grille and emblem signify its commitment to elegance and performance. The polished finish, like a mirror reflecting aspirations, mirrors the car's essence of style and speed.

However, the LF-A Concept's importance transcends its captivating exterior. Beneath the surface lies a world of cutting-edge technology and engineering brilliance. This concept car introduced groundbreaking features such as a high-revving V10 engine and lightweight materials, revealing Lexus's relentless pursuit of innovation. Its fusion of speed and precision paved the way for Lexus's future endeavors in creating vehicles that redefine luxury and driving dynamics.

2005 LEXUS LF-A CONCEPT

In 2005, the Lexus LF-A Concept made its unforgettable debut, captivating enthusiasts with its blend of form and function. Its influence, however, extended well beyond its initial unveiling. The LF-A Concept's design language and technological innovations influenced the direction of Lexus's production vehicles, shaping the brand's approach to creating high-performance cars that seamlessly blend sophistication with speed.

As you conjure the image of the 2005 Lexus LF-A Concept, let it fuel your own aspirations to fuse innovation with performance in your endeavors. Let it remind you that true greatness often involves pushing boundaries and embracing challenges to redefine what's possible. Just as the LF-A Concept's pursuit of design elegance and engineering excellence influenced Lexus's journey, so too can your audacious spirit shape the trajectory of your dreams. Its legacy isn't limited to its captivating design or powerful engine; it's a testament to the idea that the fusion of passion, engineering, and courage can create masterpieces that inspire us to accelerate towards our aspirations.

49

2006 Lamborghini Miura Concept

Imagine a world where passion for speed and design meld into an exquisite masterpiece, where innovation and elegance merge on the open road. In this realm of automotive dreams, the Lamborghini Miura Concept emerges as a symphony of power and beauty, a concept car that doesn't just capture the past, but brings it roaring into the present with a modern touch.

Picture an era when supercars were born out of audacious vision, and the road became a playground for daring engineering. In this era of automotive allure, the Lamborghini Miura Concept takes its place – a creation that doesn't merely honor history, but redefines it with contemporary flair. Conceived by the visionary minds at Lamborghini, this concept car embodies a philosophy of fusing heritage with innovation.

The Miura Concept's design is an embodiment of sensuous curves and striking presence, a marriage of form and function that ignites both the heart and the wind's embrace. Its low, sweeping profile exudes an air of speed and modernity, while the iconic headlights and bold lines hint at its legendary lineage. The sleek finish, like a reflection of desires, mirrors the car's essence of style and power.

Yet, the Miura Concept's significance reaches far beyond its captivating exterior. Beneath its sculpted surface lies a world of cutting-edge technology and engineering prowess. This concept car reintroduced the world to Lamborghini's commitment to pushing performance boundaries, featuring a potent V12 engine and advanced aerodynamics. Its blend of timeless design and modern engineering set the stage for Lamborghini's future endeavors in crafting supercars that redefine speed and aesthetics.

2006 LAMBORGHINI MIURA CONCEPT

In 2006, the Lamborghini Miura Concept made its entrancing entrance, captivating enthusiasts with its blend of form and function. Its influence, however, resonated beyond its initial unveiling. The Miura Concept's design philosophy and performance prowess found their way into Lamborghini's production vehicles, shaping the brand's approach to creating high-performance vehicles that blend heritage with innovation.

As you envision the Lamborghini Miura Concept, let it ignite your own aspirations to blend history with modernity in your pursuits. Let it remind you that true greatness often involves respecting the past while embracing the spirit of progress. Just as the Miura Concept's pursuit of design elegance and engineering excellence influenced Lamborghini's journey, so too can your audacious spirit shape the trajectory of your dreams. Its legacy isn't confined to its breathtaking design or potent engine; it's a testament to the idea that the fusion of passion, engineering, and courage can create masterpieces that inspire us to accelerate towards our aspirations.

50

2006 Saab Aero-X Concept

Picture yourself in a world where cars don't just take you from point A to B; they transport you into the realm of science fiction. In this world, the Saab Aero-X Concept emerges, a vehicle that looks like it was crafted by extraterrestrial engineers with an artistic flair.

Released in 2006, the Saab Aero-X is an embodiment of the avant-garde spirit, blending cutting-edge technology with a design that seems to defy the laws of physics. From the moment you lay eyes on it, you're transported into a realm where the future meets the present.

At first glance, the Aero-X appears to be a fighter jet without wings. Its cockpit-style canopy, hinged to open upwards like a spaceship, beckons you to enter. The body is a symphony of fluid lines and sharp angles, with a curvaceous front end that seamlessly flows into the angular rear, resembling something akin to a predator in mid-pounce.

But it's not just its striking aesthetics that make the Aero-X iconic. Underneath the sleek skin lies a powerhouse of innovation. The concept is powered by a 2.8-liter twin-turbocharged V6 engine, designed to run on 100% ethanol, showcasing Saab's commitment to sustainability. It produces a staggering 400 horsepower, propelling this beauty from 0 to 60 mph in a mere 4.9 seconds.

Yet, what truly captivates is the cockpit. The single, central driver's seat is flanked by a holographic-style head-up display that projects crucial information into the driver's line of sight. The dashboard has been stripped of traditional clutter, leaving a minimalist design that feels more like a spaceship's command center than a car interior.

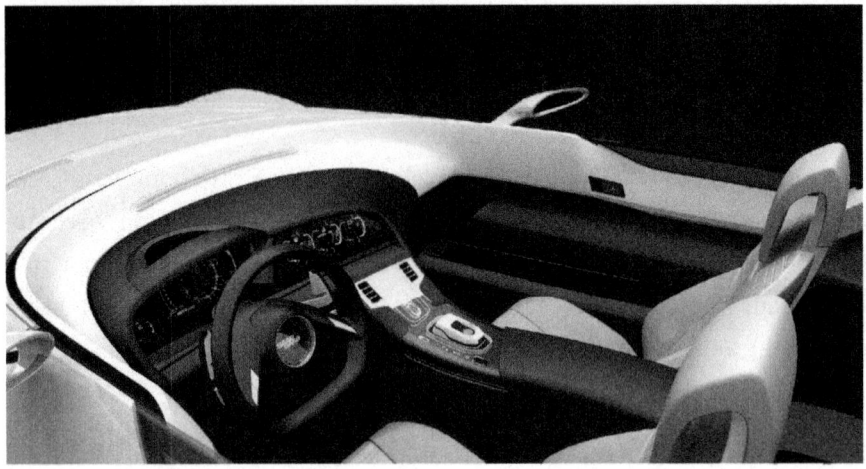

While the Saab Aero-X never made it to mass production, its influence on the automotive world is palpable. The design elements, from the aircraft-inspired canopy to the streamlined body, have found their way into various Saab production models. Moreover, its innovative approach to sustainable performance set a precedent for the industry, influencing the development of hybrid and alternative fuel vehicles.

In essence, the Saab Aero-X Concept is a testament to what can happen when imagination meets engineering prowess. It's a reminder that the automotive world is a canvas for innovation, where even the most unconventional ideas can inspire the future of mobility. This concept car is not just a glimpse into an alternative future; it's an invitation to dream beyond the limits of the road.

51

2007 BMW Concept CS

Imagine a world where luxury and performance converge, where the road transforms into a canvas for a symphony of elegance and power. In this realm of automotive aspiration, the BMW Concept CS emerges as a harmonious blend of sophistication and innovation, a concept car that doesn't just redefine the boundaries of luxury, but sets them on a thrilling new trajectory.

Picture an era when automotive design dared to break conventions, and engineering prowess was the compass guiding progress. In this era of daring exploration, the BMW Concept CS takes its place – a creation that doesn't merely push the envelope, but reshapes it with an artful touch. Brought to life by the visionary minds at BMW, this concept car embodies a philosophy of merging luxury with dynamic excellence.

The Concept CS's design is an embodiment of graceful curves and commanding presence, a fusion of form and function that captures both the eye's attention and the wind's embrace. Its sweeping lines and sculpted surfaces exude an air of sophistication and modernity, while the signature kidney grille and iconic BMW emblem hint at its legacy. The lustrous finish, like a masterpiece of desire, mirrors the car's essence of style and performance.

Yet, the Concept CS's significance goes far beyond its captivating exterior. Beneath its sculpted surface lies a realm of advanced technology and engineering brilliance. This concept car showcased BMW's commitment to pushing design boundaries, featuring innovative materials and cutting-edge aerodynamics. Its blend of luxury and performance foreshadowed the brand's future approach to creating vehicles that embody elegance and power.

2007 BMW CONCEPT CS

In 2007, the BMW Concept CS made its awe-inspiring debut, captivating enthusiasts with its blend of form and function. Its influence, however, echoed beyond its initial unveiling. The Concept CS's design language and innovative technologies found their way into BMW's production vehicles, shaping the brand's approach to crafting luxury cars that redefine opulence and driving dynamics.

As you conjure the image of the BMW Concept CS, let it inspire your own pursuits of blending luxury with innovation. Let it remind you that true greatness often involves reimagining what's possible while embracing the essence of elegance. Just as the Concept CS's pursuit of luxury and groundbreaking design influenced BMW's journey, so too can your audacious spirit shape the trajectory of your dreams. Its legacy isn't confined to its striking design or advanced materials; it's a testament to the idea that the fusion of passion, engineering, and courage can shape industries and inspire us to accelerate towards our aspirations.

52

2008 Cadillac CTS Coupe Concept

Imagine a world where elegance and power converge, where the road becomes a canvas for the fusion of artistry and engineering. In this realm of automotive dreams, the 2008 Cadillac CTS Coupe Concept emerges as a symphony of style and performance, a concept car that doesn't just redefine luxury, but reshapes it into a masterpiece of innovation.

Picture an era when automotive design wasn't just about function, but a statement of personal expression. In this era of daring imagination, the 2008 Cadillac CTS Coupe Concept takes its place – a creation that doesn't merely follow trends, but sets them with a bold stroke of American luxury. Crafted by the visionary minds at Cadillac, this concept car embodies a philosophy of fusing form with function.

The CTS Coupe Concept's design is a balance of sculpted lines and captivating presence, a fusion of aesthetics and aerodynamics that captures both the eye's attention and the wind's embrace. Its low-slung profile exudes an air of sophistication and modernity, while the iconic grille and emblem announce its premium heritage. The gleaming finish, like a reflection of aspiration, mirrors the car's essence of style and power.

Yet, the CTS Coupe Concept's influence reaches beyond its captivating exterior. Beneath its artful surface lies a world of advanced technology and engineering brilliance. This concept car introduced innovative features like advanced infotainment systems and cutting-edge safety technologies, showcasing Cadillac's dedication to pushing the boundaries of luxury and innovation. Its blend of elegance and modern tech set the stage for Cadillac's future endeavors in crafting vehicles that redefine sophistication and connectivity.

In 2008, the Cadillac CTS Coupe Concept made its stunning debut, captivating enthusiasts with its blend of form and function. Its influence, however, didn't stop at the concept stage. The CTS Coupe Concept's design cues and innovative technologies found their way into Cadillac's production vehicles, shaping the brand's approach to creating luxury cars that seamlessly blend style, performance, and cutting-edge technology.

As you conjure the image of the 2008 Cadillac CTS Coupe Concept, let it inspire your own pursuits of blending aesthetics with innovation in your endeavors. Let it remind you that true greatness often involves creating something that is not just beautiful to look at, but also advanced in its technology. Just as the CTS Coupe Concept's pursuit of design elegance and technological excellence influenced Cadillac's journey, so too can your audacious spirit shape the trajectory of your dreams. Its legacy isn't confined to its striking design or advanced features; it's a testament to the idea that the fusion of passion, engineering, and courage can shape industries and inspire us to accelerate towards our aspirations.

53

2009 Aston Martin One-77 Prototype

Picture a realm where luxury and performance unite in perfect harmony, where the road becomes a canvas for the symphony of elegance and power. In this world of automotive dreams, the 2009 Aston Martin One-77 Prototype emerges as a masterpiece of exclusivity and innovation, a concept car that doesn't just redefine luxury, but elevates it to a realm of unparalleled excellence.

Imagine an era when automotive craftsmanship transcended mere mechanics and design was a language of beauty. In this era of boundless creativity, the 2009 Aston Martin One-77 Prototype takes its place – a creation that isn't just a car, but a work of art in motion. Born from the visionary minds at Aston Martin, this concept car embodies a philosophy of blending form with function, luxury with performance.

The One-77 Prototype's design is a tapestry of sweeping curves and sculpted elegance, a fusion of aesthetics and aerodynamics that captivates both the eye's admiration and the wind's embrace. Its low, aggressive stance exudes an air of power and modernity, while the iconic Aston Martin grille and emblem whisper of its illustrious heritage. The lustrous finish, like a reflection of aspirations, mirrors the car's essence of style and performance.

Yet, the One-77 Prototype's significance extends far beyond its breathtaking exterior. Beneath its beautifully crafted skin lies a realm of cutting-edge technology and engineering brilliance. This concept car showcased Aston Martin's unwavering dedication to pushing the boundaries of design, featuring a potent V12 engine and advanced carbon-fiber construction. Its blend of luxury and performance set the stage for Aston Martin's future endeavors in crafting vehicles that redefine exclusivity and speed.

2009 ASTON MARTIN ONE-77 PROTOTYPE

In 2009, the Aston Martin One-77 Prototype made its mesmerizing debut, captivating enthusiasts with its blend of form and function. Its influence, however, echoed beyond its initial unveiling. The One-77 Prototype's design elements and technological innovations found their way into Aston Martin's production vehicles, shaping the brand's approach to creating high-performance cars that blend sophistication with speed.

As you envision the 2009 Aston Martin One-77 Prototype, let it kindle your own desires to blend luxury with innovation in your pursuits. Let it remind you that true greatness often involves crafting something that transcends the ordinary, merging beauty with power. Just as the One-77 Prototype's pursuit of design elegance and engineering excellence influenced Aston Martin's journey, so too can your audacious spirit shape the trajectory of your dreams. Its legacy isn't confined to its stunning design or powerful engine; it's a testament to the idea that the fusion of passion, engineering, and courage can create masterpieces that inspire us to accelerate towards our aspirations.

54

2009 Chevrolet Corvette Stingray Concept

Imagine a world where innovation and heritage dance together, where the road becomes a canvas for the fusion of tradition and technology. In this realm of automotive dreams, the Chevrolet Corvette Stingray Concept emerges as a harmonious blend of nostalgia and innovation, a concept car that doesn't just pay homage to the past, but propels it into the future with a modern roar.

2009 CHEVROLET CORVETTE STINGRAY CONCEPT

Picture an era when iconic designs set the stage for automotive legends, and innovation was the driving force of progress. In this era of imaginative exploration, the Chevrolet Corvette Stingray Concept takes center stage – a creation that doesn't merely recall history, but reimagines it for the modern era. Conceived by the visionary minds at Chevrolet, this concept car embodies a philosophy of embracing heritage while embracing the cutting edge.

The Stingray Concept's design is an embodiment of aggression and sculpted elegance, a fusion of form and function that captures both the eye's attention and the wind's embrace. Its sleek, low-slung profile exudes an air of speed and modernity, while the iconic split rear window and sharp lines hint at its legendary roots. The lustrous finish, like a tribute to timelessness, mirrors the car's essence of performance and innovation.

Yet, the Stingray Concept's significance extends far beyond its captivating exterior. Beneath its sculpted surface lies a realm of groundbreaking technology and engineering brilliance. This concept car introduced innovative features like advanced aerodynamics and a performance-focused hybrid powertrain, showcasing Chevrolet's dedication to pushing the boundaries of design and performance. Its blend of tradition and modernity served as a testament to the brand's commitment to evolving while honoring its legacy.

In 2009, the Chevrolet Corvette Stingray Concept made its electrifying debut, captivating enthusiasts with its blend of form and function. Its influence, however, resonated beyond its initial unveiling. The Stingray Concept's design elements and innovative technologies found their way into Chevrolet's production vehicles, shaping the brand's approach to crafting sports cars that redefine speed and aesthetics.

As you conjure the image of the Chevrolet Corvette Stingray Concept, let it spark your own aspirations to blend history with innovation in your pursuits. Let it remind you that true greatness often involves honoring the past while pushing towards the future. Just as the Stingray Concept's pursuit of heritage and groundbreaking technology influenced Chevrolet's journey, so too can your audacious spirit shape the trajectory of your dreams. Its legacy isn't confined to its striking design or hybrid powertrain; it's a testament to the idea that the fusion of passion, engineering, and courage can shape industries and inspire us to accelerate towards our aspirations.

55

2010 Jaguar C-X75

In the realm of automotive dreams, where sleek lines and roaring engines meet cutting-edge technology, there exists a masterpiece known as the

Jaguar C-X75. This concept car, born from the iconic British brand, is not just a vehicle; it's a work of art, a testament to innovation, and a symbol of Jaguar's relentless pursuit of excellence.

Imagine a car that embodies the spirit of a feline predator, poised to pounce on the road with grace and power. The Jaguar C-X75 is not just a car; it's a symphony of design, engineering, and performance, a piece of automotive artistry that pushes the boundaries of what's possible.

Unveiled in 2010 at the Paris Motor Show, the C-X75 made a grand entrance into the world of concept cars. Its design is a harmonious blend of aerodynamic prowess and elegance, with flowing lines and a sculpted body that hints at the sheer power within. But what truly sets the C-X75 apart is what lies beneath its beautiful exterior.

This concept car is powered by a hybrid drivetrain that includes not one, but two powerful electric motors, one at each axle, along with a high-revving, turbocharged 1.6-liter four-cylinder engine. Together, they produce a staggering 850 horsepower, propelling the C-X75 from 0 to 60 mph in just 2.8 seconds.

2010 JAGUAR C-X75

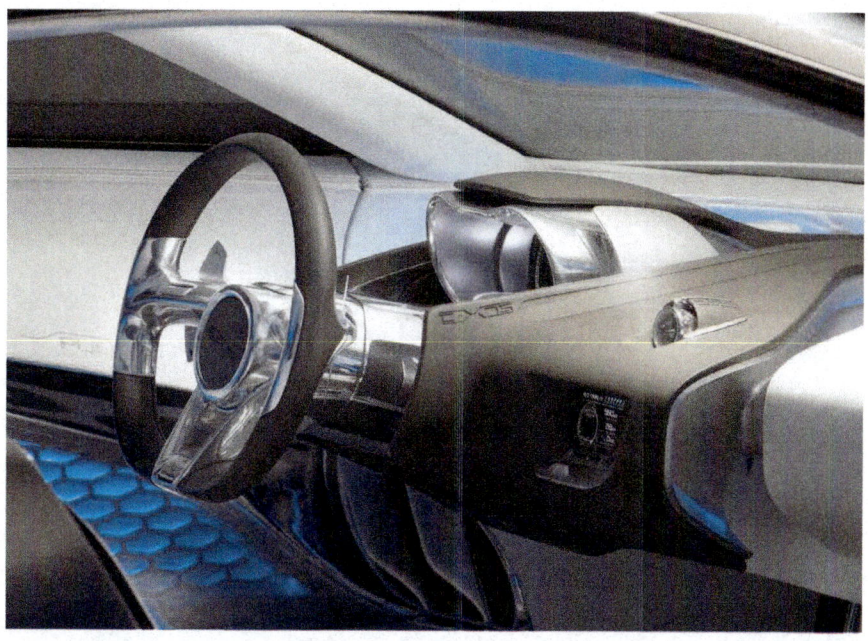

While the C-X75 itself did not make it to mass production, it left an indelible mark on the automotive world. Its advanced hybrid technology, developed in collaboration with Williams Advanced Engineering, influenced Jaguar's future production cars, including the electric I-PACE.

As you envision the Jaguar C-X75, let it remind you that the pursuit of excellence knows no bounds. It's a symbol of Jaguar's commitment to pushing the envelope of innovation, where artistry and engineering come together to create something truly extraordinary. In the world of cars, the C-X75 stands as a beacon of inspiration, a reminder that the road to the future is paved with innovation, elegance, and the relentless pursuit of automotive perfection.

56

2010 Audi Quattro Concept

Imagine a car that blends the heritage of a legendary rally champion with the sophistication of a modern-day luxury vehicle. Enter the Audi Quattro Concept, a car that not only pays homage to its iconic ancestor but also propels us into the future of automotive excellence.

2010 AUDI QUATTRO CONCEPT

Released in 2010, the Audi Quattro Concept is a testament to Audi's commitment to innovation and performance. It's not just a car; it's a bridge between the past and the future of automotive design and engineering.

The first thing that strikes you is its design. The Quattro Concept retains the spirit of the original Audi Quattro, the rally car that dominated the motorsport scene in the 1980s. Its bold, angular lines and flared wheel arches pay tribute to the original Quattro's aggressive styling, while a modern interpretation adds a touch of sophistication. This car is a nod to Audi's glorious rallying history and a promise of its high-performance future.

But the Quattro Concept is not just about nostalgia. Under the hood, it showcases Audi's prowess in cutting-edge technology. It boasts a hybrid powertrain that combines a powerful turbocharged five-cylinder engine with an electric motor. This marriage of traditional high-performance combustion and eco-friendly electric power results in thrilling acceleration and reduced emissions. Audi's Quattro all-wheel-drive system ensures that power is distributed to all four wheels, delivering superb grip and handling in all conditions.

Stepping inside, you're enveloped in a cockpit of luxury and advanced tech. The interior seamlessly merges modern minimalism with classic sportiness. Audi's innovative MMI infotainment system and a futuristic instrument cluster keep the driver connected while still focusing on the pure joy of driving.

What's particularly fascinating about the Quattro Concept is its influence on Audi's production lineup. While this exact concept may not have made it to mass production, its technological innovations and design cues have left an indelible mark on Audi's lineup. Elements like hybrid powertrains, all-wheel-drive systems, and the marriage of performance with sustainability have become integral parts of Audi's brand identity.

In the end, the Audi Quattro Concept serves as a beacon, guiding Audi's journey into the future of performance and sustainability. It reminds us that automotive excellence is not bound by time but is an ever-evolving quest, where the echoes of the past inspire the innovations of tomorrow. It's a car that stands as a testament to Audi's unwavering commitment to pushing the boundaries of what's possible in the world of automobiles.

57

2011 Chevrolet Miray Concept

Behold, the Chevrolet Miray Concept, a sleek, aerodynamic masterpiece that seamlessly blends the past, the present, and the future. Imagine a car that doesn't just transport you; it catapults you into a realm of automotive wonder.

In 2011, Chevrolet unleashed this breathtaking concept car, fusing cutting-edge technology with an homage to the brand's iconic sports cars of yesteryears. The Miray is more than just a vehicle; it's a work of art on wheels, designed to ignite your senses and set your heart racing.

Its name, "Miray," is a fusion of two Korean words: "mi," meaning future, and "ray," signifying the sun. And indeed, this concept car radiates with a futuristic glow that hints at the dawn of a new era in automotive design.

From the moment you lay eyes on the Miray, you're greeted by its striking silhouette. The low, sweeping roofline, reminiscent of a fighter jet's cockpit, hints at the car's performance pedigree. The double-bubble canopy, a nod to classic racing cars, adds a touch of nostalgia while keeping the car's modernistic spirit intact.

What truly sets the Miray apart is its forward-thinking technology. It's a plug-in hybrid electric vehicle (PHEV) that combines a 1.5-liter turbocharged gasoline engine with two front-mounted electric motors. This hybrid powertrain not only delivers exhilarating performance but also reduces emissions, a testament to Chevrolet's commitment to a sustainable automotive future.

The Miray's interior is a futuristic cocoon of luxury. Its digital cockpit seamlessly integrates cutting-edge technology, providing the driver with vital information while maintaining an uncluttered, minimalist aesthetic. The sporty, sculpted seats wrap around you, promising a thrilling driving experience.

2011 CHEVROLET MIRAY CONCEPT

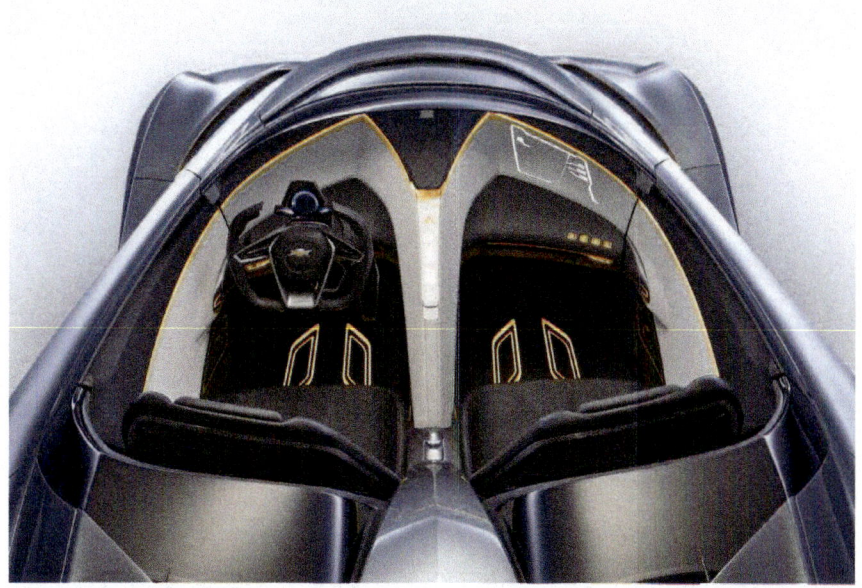

While the Miray itself didn't make it to production, its influence on Chevrolet's design philosophy is undeniable. Elements of its striking design, such as the bold front grille and the sleek, sculpted lines, have found their way into Chevrolet's mass-produced models, connecting the brand's heritage with its vision for the future.

In essence, the Chevrolet Miray Concept is a beacon of inspiration. It dares us to dream, to envision a world where performance and sustainability coexist harmoniously. It reminds us that the spirit of innovation burns brightly in the heart of Chevrolet, pushing the boundaries of what's possible in the world of automobiles.

58

2011 BMW i8 Concept

Imagine a glimpse into the future of driving – a world where innovation and sustainability dance in perfect harmony, where the road is a canvas for both style and environmental consciousness. In this realm of automotive evolution, the BMW i8 Concept emerges as a vision that transcends boundaries, a concept car that doesn't just redefine performance, but reimagines it for a new era.

Picture a moment when luxury and sustainability converge to create a car that's not just an automobile, but a statement of environmental responsibility. In this era of conscious design, the BMW i8 Concept takes its place – a creation that embodies the essence of "Born Electric." Crafted by the visionary minds at BMW, this concept car embodies a philosophy of pushing beyond the limits of convention.

The i8 Concept's design is a marriage of aerodynamics and elegance, a blend of aesthetics and efficiency that captures both the eye's admiration and the wind's embrace. Its sleek, futuristic profile speaks of innovation and modernity, while the distinctive kidney grille and LED lights symbolize BMW's commitment to style and sustainability. The striking finish, like a glimpse of tomorrow, reflects the car's essence of cutting-edge technology and eco-friendliness.

However, the i8 Concept's significance reaches far beyond its captivating exterior. Underneath its elegant shell lies a world of groundbreaking technology and engineering brilliance. This concept car introduced the world to BMW's pioneering approach to hybrid power, combining an electric motor with a high-performance gasoline engine. Its fusion of electric efficiency and dynamic performance paved the way for BMW's future endeavors in creating vehicles that redefine driving dynamics without compromising on sustainability.

In 2011, the BMW i8 Concept made its groundbreaking debut, captivating enthusiasts with its blend of form and function. Its influence, however, didn't halt at the concept stage. The i8 Concept's innovative technologies and design cues found their way into BMW's production vehicles, shaping the brand's approach to creating high-performance cars that seamlessly merge eco-friendliness with luxury.

As you conjure the image of the BMW i8 Concept, let it inspire your own aspirations to combine innovation with sustainability in your endeavors. Let it remind you that true greatness often involves pushing the boundaries of what's possible while caring for the planet we share. Just as the i8 Concept's pursuit of design elegance and engineering excellence influenced BMW's journey, so too can your audacious spirit shape the trajectory of your dreams. Its legacy isn't confined to its captivating design or advanced technology; it's a testament to the idea that the fusion of passion, engineering, and responsibility can lead us towards a future where luxury and sustainability coexist in harmony.

59

2011 Mercedes-Benz Silver Lightning

Ladies and gentlemen, in the world of automotive design and innovation, there are concept cars, and then there's the Mercedes-Benz Silver Lightning. Picture a car that doesn't just drive but glides, a machine that seems to have emerged from the future, and you'll find yourself in the presence of this electrifying masterpiece.

Released in the year 2011, the Mercedes-Benz Silver Lightning is the epitome of a concept car that transcends the ordinary. This four-wheeled work of art was designed to showcase not just the future of electric mobility but the very soul of Mercedes-Benz's commitment to innovation.

Let's dive into its captivating design. The Silver Lightning's exterior is a marvel of both form and function. Its flowing, sinuous lines resemble a lightning bolt frozen in motion, evoking a sense of power and dynamism. The car's bodywork is constructed from a material known as "liquid metal," giving it an otherworldly, almost liquid-like appearance.

But the real magic of the Silver Lightning lies under its skin. This concept car was conceived as an all-electric vehicle, powered by a quartet of in-wheel electric motors. These motors are capable of producing a staggering 740 horsepower, catapulting this lightning bolt on wheels from 0 to 60 mph in under five seconds. Imagine the thrill of such instantaneous acceleration, all with zero emissions.

Now, here's where the Silver Lightning's visionary design truly shines. It featured a "recharging lane" system, a concept that envisioned a future where highways could wirelessly charge electric vehicles as they drove. The car's unique "Silver Arrow" design was inspired by vintage racers, and its futuristic interpretation hinted at the marriage of classic beauty and future technology.

Although the Silver Lightning itself never made it into mass production, its influence on Mercedes-Benz's electric vehicle endeavors cannot be overstated. Elements of its design, from its elegant lines to its high-performance electric powertrain, have found their way into the brand's current lineup of electric vehicles. In essence, the Silver Lightning served as a beacon, illuminating the path toward a cleaner, more electrified automotive future.

In the automotive world, the Mercedes-Benz Silver Lightning is more than just a car; it's a testament to the boundless imagination of designers and engineers, a symbol of innovation, and a reminder that sometimes, the future arrives faster than we can imagine. It embodies the philosophy that to create something truly extraordinary, one must be willing to push the boundaries of what's possible.

60

2012 Lexus LF-LC Concept

Picture a car that seems to have been plucked straight from a science fiction utopia, where elegance meets innovation in a harmonious dance of automotive artistry. This is the Lexus LF-LC Concept, a beacon of avant-garde design and cutting-edge technology.

Unveiled in 2012, the LF-LC Concept isn't just a car; it's a testament to Lexus' ambition to redefine luxury and performance. Its name, LF-LC, stands for Lexus Future-Luxury Coupe, and it indeed envisions a future where luxury is reimagined, and performance is electrifying.

At first glance, you're captivated by its design. The LF-LC is a striking blend of sensual curves and sharp angles, a harmonious contradiction that works beautifully. Its spindle grille, a hallmark of Lexus design, takes center stage, exuding an aura of confidence and sophistication. The sweeping roofline flows seamlessly into the sculpted rear, creating an aerodynamic masterpiece. The LF-LC is a sculpture on wheels, a rolling work of art that turns heads wherever it goes.

But what truly sets the LF-LC apart is what lies beneath its sculpted skin. This concept car boasts a hybrid powertrain that combines a high-performance V8 engine with an advanced electric motor. The result is not just power but efficiency, a symphony of combustion and electricity working together to deliver thrilling performance with reduced environmental impact. Lexus was showcasing its commitment to sustainability without compromising on the exhilaration of driving.

Step inside, and you're enveloped in a cabin that is a blend of opulence and innovation. The interior showcases a combination of leather, suede, and advanced materials, creating a luxurious yet futuristic ambiance. A massive touchscreen interface dominates the dashboard, seamlessly integrating infotainment and vehicle control.

The LF-LC Concept, while not a production vehicle, has significantly influenced Lexus' lineup. Elements like the spindle grille and hybrid powertrains have become signatures of the brand, featured in many of its mass-production models. Lexus took the spirit of innovation and applied it to their entire range, elevating the driving experience for all their customers.

In summary, the Lexus LF-LC Concept is a visionary work of art, a glimpse into a future where luxury and performance seamlessly coexist. It's a reminder that automotive design can be both a source of inspiration and a catalyst for change, pushing the boundaries of what's possible. This concept car represents Lexus' commitment to crafting not just cars, but experiences that transcend the ordinary, making every journey a masterpiece.

61

2012 Honda NSX Concept

Imagine a sleek and powerful beast, poised at the intersection of art and engineering, waiting to redefine the very essence of what a sports car can be. This is the Honda NSX Concept, a true embodiment of innovation and performance.

The year is 2012, and the automotive world is buzzing with anticipation as Honda unveils the NSX Concept. It's not just a car; it's a statement, a testament to Honda's commitment to pushing the boundaries of automotive design and technology.

At first glance, you're struck by its low, aerodynamic silhouette, a form that seems to slice through the air effortlessly. Every curve and contour is meticulously designed, not just for aesthetics but to enhance performance. This is a car that marries beauty and purpose in a harmonious dance.

Step inside, and you'll find a driver-focused cockpit that blends cutting-edge technology with a minimalist, elegant design. The NSX Concept's cabin is a place where the driver and the machine become one. It's an ode to the purity of the driving experience, where every control and interface is at your fingertips, perfectly calibrated for exhilarating precision.

Underneath its sculpted exterior lies the heart of a hybrid powertrain, a groundbreaking concept at the time. The NSX Concept combines a V6 engine with not one, but three electric motors, creating a "Sport Hybrid Super Handling All-Wheel Drive" system. This innovative technology doesn't just deliver breathtaking acceleration; it also enhances cornering capabilities, providing a level of control and agility previously unseen in a sports car.

The NSX Concept was a promise of things to come. It represented Honda's commitment to sustainable, high-performance driving, a vision that would ultimately materialize in the production version of the NSX. In 2016, the world witnessed the rebirth of an icon, as the all-new Acura NSX (badged as Acura for the North American market) hit the streets.

The influence of the NSX Concept extended far beyond its own production. It inspired a new era of hybrid sports cars, where environmental consciousness and heart-pounding performance could coexist. Today, we see hybrid and electric technologies being embraced by many automakers as they strive to capture the spirit of innovation that the NSX Concept first embodied.

In the world of automotive design and performance, the Honda NSX Concept remains a symbol of what's possible when visionary thinking meets cutting-edge technology. It's a reminder that the pursuit of excellence knows no bounds and that a single concept car can ignite a revolution that forever changes the automotive landscape.

62

2013 Nissan IDx

Picture a journey into the realm of automotive nostalgia – a place where modern innovation meets the timeless charm of classic design. In this captivating world of automotive imagination, the Nissan IDx emerges as a bridge between eras, a concept car that channels the spirit of the past while embracing the technologies of the future.

Imagine a moment when the past and the present harmonize to create a car that's not just an automobile, but a celebration of heritage and innovation. In this era of modern-retro fusion, the Nissan IDx takes its place – a creation that pays homage to legendary Nissan models while embarking on a new path of design and technology. Crafted by the visionary minds at Nissan, this concept car represents a blend of nostalgia and forward-thinking.

The IDx's design is a tapestry of vintage aesthetics and contemporary lines, a fusion of timeless charm and modern flair that captures both the eye's admiration and the road's embrace. Its compact yet bold profile evokes a sense of agility and excitement, while design elements reminiscent of classic Datsun and Nissan models pay homage to the brand's storied history. The pristine finish, like a window to the past and future, mirrors the car's essence of style and innovation.

Yet, the IDx's significance reaches beyond its captivating exterior. Underneath its retro-inspired skin lies a world of innovative technologies and engineering brilliance. This concept car showcased Nissan's commitment to marrying heritage with modernity, while the integration of advanced connectivity features and efficient powertrains highlighted the brand's vision for the future. Its blend of nostalgic design cues and cutting-edge technology set a new standard for Nissan's approach to creating vehicles that honor the past while embracing the present.

In 2013, the Nissan IDx made its enchanting debut, captivating enthusiasts with its unique blend of form and function. Its influence, however, didn't remain confined to the concept stage. While the IDx itself didn't transition to mass production, its design philosophy and innovative ideas found their way into Nissan's production vehicles, shaping the brand's approach to creating cars that resonate with a new generation while respecting the brand's legacy.

As you conjure the image of the Nissan IDx, let it inspire your own aspirations to blend tradition with innovation in your endeavors. Let it remind you that true greatness often involves drawing inspiration from the past while embracing the possibilities of the future. Just as the IDx's pursuit of nostalgic design and forward-thinking technology influenced Nissan's journey, so too can your audacious spirit shape the trajectory of your dreams. Its legacy isn't limited to its captivating design or innovative features; it's a testament to the idea that the fusion of heritage, engineering, and creativity can shape industries and inspire us to accelerate towards our aspirations.

63

2013 Mercedes-Benz AMG Vision Gran Turismo

Imagine a world where the boundaries of imagination merge seamlessly with the realm of automotive excellence. In this exhilarating realm, the

2013 MERCEDES-BENZ AMG VISION GRAN TURISMO

Mercedes-Benz AMG Vision Gran Turismo emerges as a work of art that blurs the lines between dreams and reality, a concept car that transcends the ordinary and propels us into a future where design and performance intertwine.

Visualize a moment when design becomes a language of pure emotion, a fusion of power and aesthetics that ignites the senses. In this era of expressive creativity, the Mercedes-Benz AMG Vision Gran Turismo takes its place – not just as a car, but as a testament to the pursuit of automotive perfection. Crafted by the masterful hands at Mercedes-Benz, this concept car embodies a philosophy of pushing the limits of what's possible.

The AMG Vision Gran Turismo's design is a dance of sculpted curves and aggressive lines, a marriage of elegance and dynamism that captures both the eye's admiration and the wind's embrace. Its low, dramatic profile radiates a sense of power and futuristic allure, while the iconic Mercedes-Benz grille and gullwing doors evoke a sense of heritage and innovation. The polished finish, like a reflection of desires, mirrors the car's essence of style and performance.

Yet, the AMG Vision Gran Turismo's significance goes beyond its captivating exterior. Beneath its stunning skin lies a world of cutting-edge technology and engineering brilliance. This concept car showcased Mercedes-AMG's dedication to pushing the boundaries of design and performance, introducing innovative features like a high-performance hybrid powertrain and advanced aerodynamics. Its blend of power and innovation set a new standard for Mercedes-AMG's future endeavors in crafting vehicles that redefine driving dynamics.

In 2013, the Mercedes-Benz AMG Vision Gran Turismo made its electrifying entrance, captivating enthusiasts with its blend of form and function. While initially created for the virtual world of a popular racing video game, the concept car's influence transcended the digital realm. Design cues and performance innovations from the AMG Vision Gran Turismo found their way into Mercedes-AMG's production vehicles, shaping the brand's approach to creating high-performance cars that seamlessly blend luxury with speed.

As you conjure the image of the Mercedes-Benz AMG Vision Gran Turismo, let it inspire your own aspirations to combine design with innovation in your pursuits. Let it remind you that true greatness often involves pushing the limits of what's possible while maintaining an unwavering commitment to beauty and performance. Just as the AMG Vision Gran Turismo's pursuit of design elegance and engineering excellence influenced Mercedes-AMG's journey, so too can your audacious spirit shape the trajectory of your dreams. Its legacy isn't confined to its stunning design or powerful engine; it's a testament to the idea that the fusion of passion, engineering, and courage can shape industries and inspire us to accelerate towards our aspirations.

64

2014 Toyota FT-1

Imagine a journey into the realm of automotive dreams, where design and performance meld to create a symphony of driving passion. In this captivating world, the Toyota FT-1 stands as a masterpiece of innovation and artistry, a concept car that not only embodies the essence of pure driving excitement but also inspires us to imagine the future of sports cars.

Envision a moment when form and function unite to craft not just a vehicle, but a manifestation of speed and style. In this era of automotive exploration, the Toyota FT-1 takes center stage – not merely as a concept, but as a declaration of Toyota's commitment to redefining the sports car experience. Conceived by the ingenious minds at Toyota's Calty Design Research, this concept car represents a harmonious fusion of performance and design.

The design of the Toyota FT-1 is a fusion of flowing lines and sharp angles, a dance of aesthetics and aerodynamics that captures both the eye's admiration and the wind's embrace. Its aggressive stance exudes a sense of power and modernity, while the iconic double-bubble roof and sculpted surfaces evoke a timeless sense of speed and dynamism. The bold color choices, like brushstrokes of automotive passion, mirror the car's embodiment of speed and performance.

However, the significance of the Toyota FT-1 transcends its captivating exterior. Beneath its stunning surface lies a world of advanced technology and engineering prowess. This concept car showcases Toyota's dedication to pushing the boundaries of performance, introducing innovative features like a powerful internal combustion engine or even hybrid powertrains. Its fusion of power and innovation sets a new standard for Toyota's approach to creating vehicles that redefine the driving experience.

2014 TOYOTA FT-1

The Toyota FT-1 made its debut in 2014, captivating enthusiasts with its blend of aesthetics and performance. While not every detail transitioned directly to production, the concept's influence resonates through Toyota's lineup, guiding the development of sports cars like the Toyota GR Supra. The FT-1's legacy lives on in Toyota's relentless pursuit of creating vehicles that ignite the senses and thrill drivers.

As you envision the Toyota FT-1, let it fuel your aspirations to merge aesthetics with performance in your pursuits. Let it remind you that true greatness often involves pushing the boundaries of what's possible while embracing the beauty of design. Just as the FT-1's pursuit of performance and artistic brilliance influenced Toyota's journey, so too can your audacious spirit shape the trajectory of your dreams. Its legacy isn't confined to its powerful features or visionary design; it's a testament to the idea that the fusion of passion, engineering, and performance can shape industries and inspire us to accelerate towards our aspirations.

65

2014 Chevrolet Chaparral 2X Vision Gran Turismo

In the realm of imagination and innovation, where the racetrack meets the virtual world, there exists a machine that blurs the boundaries between reality and fantasy. This is the Chevrolet Chaparral 2X Vision Gran Turismo, a concept car born from the desire to push the limits of what's possible in the world of automotive design and technology.

Picture a car that doesn't just hug the asphalt but hugs the very essence of speed and performance. The Chevrolet Chaparral 2X is more than a car; it's an embodiment of racing's spirit, an exploration of futuristic design, and an ode to the marriage of man and machine in the pursuit of speed.

Unveiled in 2014 as part of the Vision Gran Turismo project for the popular PlayStation racing game, this concept car took the automotive world by storm. Its design is a futuristic marvel, with a cockpit that looks like it was plucked from the set of a sci-fi movie. It's low-slung, sleek, and aerodynamically optimized for one purpose: to slice through the air like a precision instrument.

But what truly sets the Chaparral 2X apart is its innovative technology. This concept car features a laser-powered propulsion system that propels it from 0 to 60 mph in a mind-boggling 1.5 seconds. It's a glimpse into a world where fossil fuels are replaced by laser beams, and where the roar of an engine is replaced by the whirr of advanced technology.

While the Chevrolet Chaparral 2X Vision Gran Turismo remains a concept car destined for the virtual racetrack, its influence on the world of automotive design and technology is palpable. It has inspired a new generation of engineers and designers to think outside the box, to dream of a future where cars not only break speed records but rewrite the rules of propulsion.

As you envision the Chevrolet Chaparral 2X, let it ignite your own passion for innovation and the pursuit of the extraordinary. Let it remind you that the future of automotive design is limited only by our imagination, and that the line between reality and fantasy can blur in the pursuit of automotive perfection. It's a testament to the idea that, in the world of cars, the future is as exciting and boundary-pushing as we dare to dream it to be.

66

2015 Bugatti Vision Gran Turismo

Close your eyes and envision a world where the boundaries of possibility dissolve into a symphony of power and artistry. In this realm of automotive dreams, the Bugatti Vision Gran Turismo emerges as a breathtaking embodiment of speed and design, a concept car that unleashes the imagination and dares to redefine the very essence of luxury performance.

Imagine a moment when engineering prowess and artistic brilliance converge to create a car that's not just an automobile, but a manifestation of velocity and elegance. In this era of automotive innovation, the Bugatti Vision Gran Turismo takes its place – not merely as a car, but as a beacon of inspiration for creators and dreamers alike. Forged by the visionary minds at Bugatti, this concept car signifies a fusion of bold ambition and technical mastery.

The Vision Gran Turismo's design is a ballet of aerodynamic shapes and cutting-edge details, a fusion of form and function that captivates both the eye and the wind. Its low-slung profile speaks of speed and modernity, while Bugatti's signature horseshoe grille and iconic curves evoke a timeless sense of grandeur and performance. The mesmerizing finish, like a glimpse of automotive tomorrow, reflects the car's essence of relentless pursuit of excellence.

Yet, the significance of the Vision Gran Turismo transcends its captivating exterior. Beneath its sculpted bodywork lies a world of awe-inspiring technology and engineering brilliance. This concept car was a canvas for Bugatti's most innovative ideas, featuring a hybrid powertrain that marries immense horsepower with environmental consciousness. Its blend of power and innovation served as a testament to Bugatti's unyielding commitment to redefining the limits of speed and luxury.

In 2015, the Bugatti Vision Gran Turismo roared into existence, captivating enthusiasts with its blend of form and function. Its influence, however, didn't end with its concept status. While not intended for mass production, the Vision Gran Turismo's design elements and technological innovations found their way into Bugatti's production vehicles, shaping the brand's approach to creating hypercars that blend heart-stopping performance with unparalleled artistry.

As you conjure the image of the Bugatti Vision Gran Turismo, let it ignite your own aspirations to infuse innovation with elegance in your endeavors. Let it remind you that true greatness often involves pushing beyond the boundaries of convention while crafting beauty and power in perfect harmony. Just as the Vision Gran Turismo's pursuit of design elegance and engineering excellence influenced Bugatti's journey, so too can your audacious spirit shape the trajectory of your dreams. Its legacy isn't confined to its exquisite design or groundbreaking technologies; it's a testament to the idea that the fusion of passion, engineering, and imagination can shape industries and inspire us to accelerate towards our aspirations.

67

2015 Porsche Mission E

Picture a world where the future of driving unfolds before your eyes, where the fusion of innovation and passion propels us into a new era of automotive excellence. In this electrifying realm, the Porsche Mission E emerges as a harbinger of electric performance and avant-garde design, a concept car that not only redefines the boundaries of electric mobility but also sets a trailblazing path towards a sustainable yet thrilling driving experience.

Imagine a moment when engineering brilliance and aesthetic mastery intertwine to give birth to not just a vehicle, but an automotive masterpiece. In this age of electrification, the Porsche Mission E takes center stage – not merely as a concept, but as a testament to Porsche's unrelenting commitment to elevating the driving journey. Forged by the ingenious minds at Porsche, this concept car symbolizes a harmonious blend of sustainable technology and exhilarating performance.

The design of the Mission E is a symphony of sleek lines and dynamic contours, a fusion of form and function that captivates both the eye and the wind. Its low, aerodynamic silhouette speaks of speed and modernity, while the iconic Porsche front fascia and signature lighting elements evoke a timeless sense of prestige and dynamism. The flawless finish, like a glimpse of automotive future, reflects the car's essence of innovation and sportiness.

However, the significance of the Mission E extends far beyond its captivating exterior. Beneath its elegant shell lies a world of groundbreaking technology and engineering ingenuity. This concept car showcases Porsche's dedication to pushing the boundaries of electric performance, introducing cutting-edge features like high-voltage charging systems and a revolutionary lithium-ion battery architecture. Its fusion of sustainable power and advanced engineering establishes a new standard for Porsche's approach to creating electric vehicles that marry luxury and high-octane thrill.

2015 PORSCHE MISSION E

In 2015, the Porsche Mission E concept graced the stage, captivating enthusiasts with its blend of form and function. While not every detail transitioned directly to production, the concept's influence reverberated through Porsche's lineup, contributing to the development of the Porsche Taycan, the brand's first all-electric production car. The Taycan, launched in 2019, embodies the ethos of the Mission E, bringing together sustainable innovation and Porsche's unrivaled driving dynamics.

As you conjure the image of the Porsche Mission E, let it spark your own aspirations to merge innovation with elegance in your pursuits. Let it remind you that true greatness often involves pushing the boundaries of what's possible while honoring a commitment to sustainability and luxury. Just as the Mission E's pursuit of groundbreaking design and engineering brilliance influenced Porsche's journey, so too can your audacious spirit shape the trajectory of your dreams. Its legacy isn't confined to its groundbreaking technologies or future-forward design; it's a testament to the idea that the fusion of passion, engineering, and vision can shape industries and inspire us to accelerate towards our aspirations.

68

2015 Aston Martin DBX Concept

Picture a car that embodies the fusion of elegance and power, a concept that redefines what it means to drive in style. In this automotive tale, we meet the Aston Martin DBX Concept, a true gem in the world of luxury SUVs.

2015 ASTON MARTIN DBX CONCEPT

Imagine standing before this beauty, a breathtaking blend of sleek, aerodynamic lines and Aston Martin's unmistakable design language. The DBX Concept, introduced in 2015, challenged the notion that SUVs were solely utilitarian vehicles. Instead, it transformed them into symbols of opulence and performance.

This concept marked a significant departure from Aston Martin's traditional sports cars, a bold step into the world of family-friendly luxury. The DBX's silhouette, with its low roofline and broad stance, exuded an air of sophistication while retaining the brand's iconic grille and athletic curves.

But what truly set the DBX Concept apart was the promise of innovative technologies. It wasn't just a stylish SUV; it was a glimpse into a future where high-performance and environmental consciousness could coexist. Electric and hybrid powertrains were considered, hinting at a commitment to sustainability without compromising on power and speed.

The DBX Concept, with its refined aesthetics and eco-conscious technologies, sent ripples through the automotive world. Luxury SUVs began incorporating similar design principles and exploring cleaner energy sources. It was a pivotal moment, signifying that even the most revered traditions in the auto industry could evolve to embrace the changing times.

Today, the Aston Martin DBX is not just a concept; it's a production reality. It represents a harmonious blend of art and engineering, a testament to the enduring appeal of innovation. As you gaze upon it, remember that it all began with a vision, the vision of the Aston Martin DBX Concept, a car that dared to reimagine what a luxury SUV could be.

69

2015 Hyundai N 2025 Vision Gran Turismo

Imagine a car that's not just from the future but a leap into the realms of science fiction. Enter the Hyundai N 2025 Vision Gran Turismo, a concept car that defies convention and invites you to dream beyond the boundaries of today's automotive world.

The year is 2015, and Hyundai unveils this otherworldly concept. It's more than just a car; it's a vision, a bold proclamation that the future of high-performance driving will be electrifying in every sense of the word.

At first glance, the N 2025 Vision Gran Turismo looks like a spacecraft that's touched down on Earth. Its low-slung, aerodynamic form seems poised for interstellar travel rather than earthly roads. The design is not just an aesthetic choice but a testament to the car's commitment to speed and efficiency. It's as if Hyundai took inspiration from the fastest fighter jets and fused it with the grace of a cheetah.

Step inside, and you're greeted by a cockpit straight out of a sci-fi movie. Every surface, every control, seems like it was lifted from a spacecraft. This is a driver's cockpit where technology and man become one. From the holographic HUD to the multifunctional steering wheel, the N 2025 is a vision of how future cars could be.

Beneath its stunning exterior is an advanced hydrogen fuel cell powertrain. Hyundai envisioned a world where high-performance cars could be environmentally friendly. The N 2025 is not just a concept; it's a bold statement about the potential of hydrogen technology in the world of performance cars.

While the N 2025 Vision Gran Turismo was created for the Gran Turismo video game series, its impact went far beyond virtual racing. It inspired Hyundai's commitment to hydrogen fuel cell technology, which we see in their production vehicles today, like the Hyundai Nexo.

This concept car serves as a reminder that the future of automotive design and performance is limited only by our imaginations. It encourages us to dream of cars that are not only faster and more efficient but also kinder to our planet. In the world of Hyundai, the N 2025 Vision Gran Turismo was not just a concept; it was a glimpse into a future where performance and sustainability coexist harmoniously.

70

2015 Mercedes-Benz F 015 Luxury in Motion

Step into the realm of automotive dreams, where the future unfolds in the most luxurious and visionary fashion. In this world, the Mercedes-Benz F 015 Luxury in Motion is not just a car; it's a marvel of innovation, a glimpse into the future of mobility, and an embodiment of luxury on wheels.

Imagine a vehicle that's not merely a mode of transport, but a cocoon of comfort and connectivity, where the very act of driving evolves into a new form of personalized luxury. The Mercedes-Benz F 015 is not bound by the confines of time; it's a concept car that pushes the boundaries of what's possible.

This concept car, unveiled in 2015, paints a picture of a future where self-driving technology takes center stage. The F 015 envisions a world where the car becomes a haven for relaxation, conversation, and work while safely navigating the road. Its design is nothing short of futuristic elegance, with sleek lines and a spacious, lounge-like interior adorned with high-end materials.

But what truly sets the F 015 apart is its vision of autonomous driving. The car can switch between manual and autonomous modes, giving passengers the choice of being in control or simply enjoying the ride. It's a mobile sanctuary where technology enables a seamless blend of work and leisure, connecting occupants to their digital lives like never before.

While the F 015 itself may not have reached mass production, its influence on the automotive industry is undeniable. It has sparked a movement towards autonomous driving and redefined the idea of in-car connectivity. Features once thought of as science fiction are now becoming reality in today's production vehicles, thanks in part to the groundbreaking vision that the F 015 represents.

As you envision the Mercedes-Benz F 015 Luxury in Motion, let it remind you that the future of mobility is not just about getting from A to B; it's about the journey itself. It's a future where technology and luxury coalesce to create a new era of automotive innovation, where the road ahead is illuminated by the promise of progress, and where the car of tomorrow is a haven of comfort, connectivity, and, above all, luxury in motion.

71

2016 MINI Vision Next 100

Step into the future of urban mobility with the MINI Vision Next 100 - a groundbreaking concept car that redefines how we think about compact vehicles. Imagine yourself in the year 2016, where MINI, renowned for its iconic small cars, introduced a concept that's not just a car but a vision for the next century of urban living.

The MINI Vision Next 100 is a testament to the brand's legacy of delivering clever and compact automobiles. It embodies MINI's philosophy of creating cars that seamlessly integrate into our bustling urban landscapes, and it pushes the boundaries of design and technology.

At first glance, you notice the futuristic yet unmistakably MINI design. It retains the iconic circular headlights, contrasting roof, and compact proportions, but there's something more - a sense of evolution. The Vision Next 100 concept foresees a world where individual car ownership may give way to communal mobility solutions.

One of the most striking features of the MINI Vision Next 100 is its autonomous driving capability. In an era where cars still required human drivers, this concept boldly envisions a world where vehicles can navigate the city on their own. Its "Cooperizer" AI ensures a personalized and stress-free journey.

The interior is a masterpiece of minimalism and adaptability. It's a flexible space that transforms to suit the driver's preferences, whether you want to take control of the wheel or let the car drive itself. This concept represents a future where cars become multifunctional, flexible environments, seamlessly integrated into our daily lives.

2016 MINI VISION NEXT 100

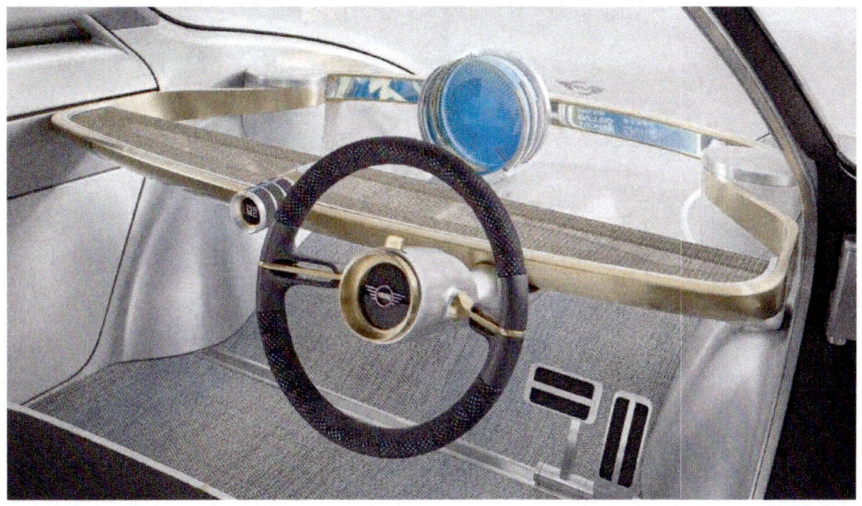

Released as part of BMW's centenary celebrations, the MINI Vision Next 100 is more than a concept car; it's a reflection of the evolving automotive landscape. Its influence on mass production cars can be seen in the continued development of autonomous and electric technologies by MINI and other manufacturers.

In essence, the MINI Vision Next 100 beckons us to reimagine the future of urban mobility. It's a bold and innovative step towards a world where cars are not just modes of transportation but integrated, intelligent companions in our fast-paced urban lives.

72

2016 BMW Vision Next 100

Imagine a world where driving is not just a mode of transportation but an art form, a world where the very act of getting behind the wheel is an immersive experience that blurs the lines between man and machine. In this captivating vision of the future, the BMW Vision Next 100 emerges as a groundbreaking concept car, a symbol of innovation, sustainability, and a redefined relationship between driver and vehicle.

Picture a moment when tradition and innovation coalesce into a harmonious masterpiece. In this era of rapid technological advancement, the BMW Vision Next 100 stands as a testament to the automaker's century-long legacy of driving pleasure and innovation. Born from a rich history of craftsmanship and performance, this concept car represents a profound shift in our understanding of mobility.

The design of the BMW Vision Next 100 is a glimpse into a future where form follows function in the most elegant and efficient way possible. Its clean, minimalist lines and seamless surfaces create an aesthetic that's both futuristic and timeless. The interior is a sanctuary of luxury and connectivity, where the driver is not just a passenger but a pilot in full control, aided by advanced AI and augmented reality.

However, the significance of the BMW Vision Next 100 goes beyond its captivating exterior and luxurious interior. This concept car showcases BMW's commitment to sustainable mobility, featuring an all-electric powertrain and autonomous driving capabilities. It envisions a world where vehicles communicate with each other and adapt to the driver's preferences, redefining the relationship between human and machine.

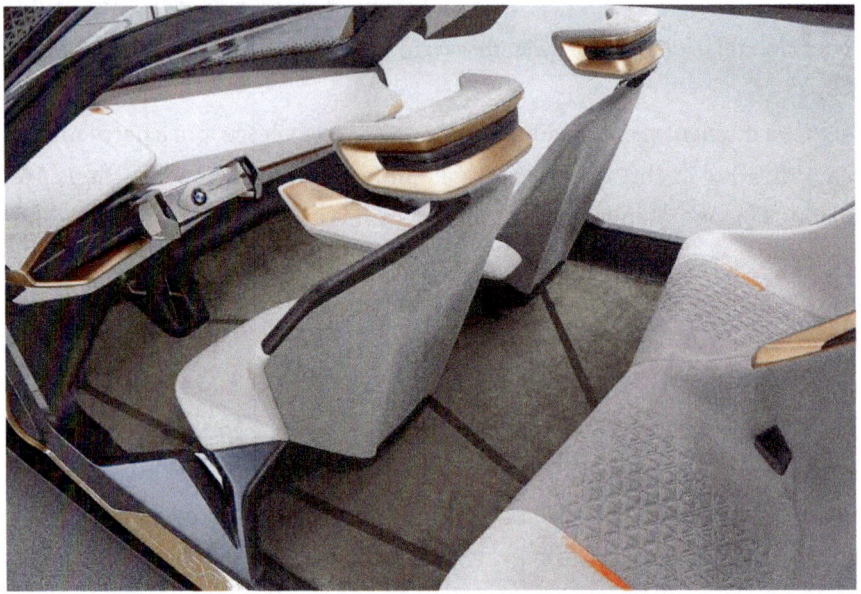

Unveiled in 2016 as part of BMW's centenary celebrations, the Vision Next 100 marked a pivotal moment in the company's history, signaling its dedication to shaping the future of mobility. While not every detail of the Vision Next 100 made it to production, its influence is evident in BMW's ongoing development of electric and autonomous vehicles. The concept's legacy lives on in BMW's unwavering pursuit of creating vehicles that embody the brand's core values of performance, innovation, and driving pleasure.

As you visualize the BMW Vision Next 100, let it inspire your own journey towards a future where tradition and innovation coexist in perfect harmony. Let it remind you that progress doesn't have to come at the expense of heritage, and that the fusion of craftsmanship, innovation, and sustainability can redefine industries and inspire us to move forward towards a more elegant and connected world. Its legacy isn't confined to its remarkable features or visionary design; it's a testament to the idea that the future of mobility is as much about the joy of driving as it is about the technology that propels us forward.

73

2016 Rolls-Royce Vision Next 100

Step into the future, a future where opulence and innovation coalesce into an automotive masterpiece - the Rolls-Royce Vision Next 100. Picture yourself in the year 2016, as Rolls-Royce, the paragon of luxury, unveiled a concept car that transcended time and space, offering a glimpse into the next century of automotive excellence.

The Rolls-Royce Vision Next 100, also known as the 103EX, is more than just a car; it's an embodiment of the brand's unwavering commitment to crafting the most exquisite and forward-thinking automobiles. This concept car, born from the marque's legacy of craftsmanship, heralded a new era of automotive design and technology.

At first glance, the Vision Next 100 is a study in elegance, an ethereal vision draped in sleek lines and sculpted curves. Its long, sweeping body conjures images of classic Rolls-Royces, while its Spirit of Ecstasy emblem takes on an illuminated, ethereal form. But this is where the familiarity ends and the future begins.

As you approach, the Vision Next 100's grand coach doors open wide, unveiling an interior that defies convention. There are no driver's or passenger's seats in the traditional sense. Instead, you find a luxurious lounge with ample space to relax, converse, and savor the journey.

The heart of this opulent vessel is its cutting-edge AI named "Eleanor." Eleanor is not just an assistant but a guardian, ensuring a seamless and safe ride. She draws inspiration from the past to anticipate your desires in the present and future, making the Vision Next 100 a truly intuitive mode of transportation.

The iconic "Pantheon" grille, a Rolls-Royce hallmark, is replaced by a breathtaking glass front, adorned with handcrafted regal details. This bold design shift exemplifies the brand's willingness to embrace innovation without sacrificing its heritage.

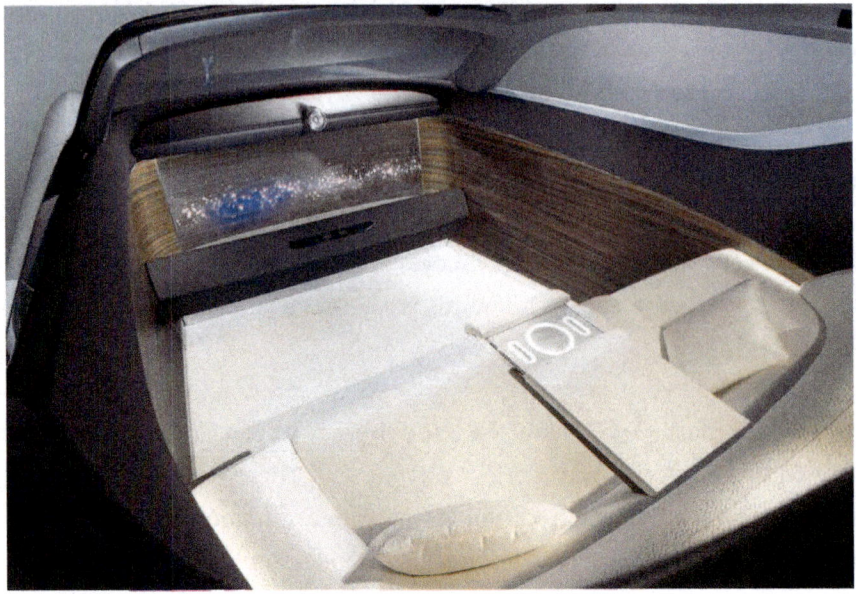

While the Vision Next 100 is a concept, it's also a harbinger of what's to come. Its influence is felt in the pursuit of electric and autonomous technology by Rolls-Royce and other automakers. The concept's commitment to an opulent and personalized journey remains a guiding principle for luxury car manufacturers in the 21st century.

In summary, the Rolls-Royce Vision Next 100 transcends the boundaries of time, offering a vision of luxury travel that marries tradition with innovation. It beckons us to dream of a future where opulence knows no bounds and where the Spirit of Ecstasy guides us into the next century of automotive excellence.

74

2016 Cadillac Escala

Close your eyes and imagine a world where automotive luxury reaches new heights, where elegance and innovation converge to create a masterpiece on wheels. In this captivating realm, the Cadillac Escala emerges as a symbol of opulence and visionary design, a concept car that not only redefines luxury but also inspires us to envision the future of sophistication and driving pleasure.

Picture a moment when artistry and engineering brilliance unite to craft not just a vehicle, but a statement of prestige and grace. In this era of automotive ingenuity, the Cadillac Escala takes center stage – not merely as a concept, but as a testament to Cadillac's unwavering commitment to elevating the driving experience. Conceived by the masterful minds at Cadillac, this concept car represents a harmonious blend of artistic elegance and cutting-edge technology.

The design of the Escala is a symphony of graceful lines and sculpted contours, a marriage of aesthetics and aerodynamics that captures both the eye's admiration and the wind's embrace. Its grand proportions exude a sense of presence and modernity, while the iconic Cadillac grille and bold lighting elements evoke a timeless sense of prestige and power. The refined finish, like a reflection of luxury's essence, mirrors the car's embodiment of sophistication and innovation.

However, the significance of the Escala transcends its captivating exterior. Beneath its exquisite surface lies a world of advanced technology and engineering excellence. This concept car showcases Cadillac's dedication to pushing the boundaries of luxury, introducing features like a twin-turbocharged V8 engine and a host of driver-centric technologies. Its fusion of opulent comfort and high-tech innovation sets a new standard for Cadillac's approach to creating vehicles that redefine luxury driving.

In 2016, the Cadillac Escala concept made its grand entrance, captivating enthusiasts with its blend of form and function. While not every aspect translated directly to production, the concept's influence resonated through Cadillac's lineup, influencing the design language and features of the brand's luxury models. The Escala's legacy lives on in Cadillac's pursuit of elevating the luxury driving experience.

As you conjure the image of the Cadillac Escala, let it ignite your own aspirations to merge luxury with innovation in your endeavors. Let it remind you that true greatness often involves a harmonious blend of artistry and technology, where opulence and functionality coexist. Just as the Escala's pursuit of elegance and engineering brilliance influenced Cadillac's journey, so too can your audacious spirit shape the trajectory of your dreams. Its legacy isn't confined to its luxurious features or visionary design; it's a testament to the idea that the fusion of passion, engineering, and sophistication can shape industries and inspire us to accelerate towards our aspirations.

75

2016 Lucid Air Concept

In the realm of automotive innovation, there are moments when a new star emerges, illuminating the path forward for the entire industry. In this story, we dive into the captivating world of the Lucid Air Concept, a groundbreaking vision that redefines luxury electric vehicles and heralds a new era of sustainable transportation.

Picture a car that glides through the wind with the grace of a whisper. The Lucid Air Concept, birthed by the American electric vehicle manufacturer Lucid Motors, is an embodiment of elegance and innovation. Released in 2016, it's more than just a car; it's a testament to the future of electric mobility.

The Lucid Air's design is nothing short of breathtaking. It marries sleek, aerodynamic lines with an aura of sophistication. Its sculpted silhouette and captivating light signatures define a design philosophy that's both futuristic and timeless. The seamless integration of technology is apparent in its flush-mounted door handles and slim LED headlights.

Beneath its elegant exterior lies a technological marvel. The Lucid Air Concept showcases the remarkable capabilities of electric power. With a range that surpasses 500 miles on a single charge, it shatters preconceived notions of EV limitations. Its electric powertrain not only provides astonishing acceleration but also delivers an incredibly smooth and quiet ride.

Step inside, and you're greeted by an interior that's a blend of opulence and minimalism. Sustainable materials and a spacious cabin create an environment where innovation and comfort coexist. The centerpiece is a 34-inch curved Glass Cockpit 5K display that seamlessly integrates with a floating center console. It's a digital haven for the tech-savvy driver.

The Lucid Air Concept has far-reaching implications for the automotive industry. It's not just a concept car; it's a bold statement that electric vehicles can combine luxury, performance, and sustainability. Its influence has inspired other automakers to rethink their approach to electric mobility, pushing boundaries in design, range, and technology.

In summary, the Lucid Air Concept is a beacon of progress in the automotive world. It's a harmonious blend of design, technology, and sustainability. Released in 2016, it serves as a reminder that innovation knows no bounds, and it's setting the stage for a future where luxury and eco-consciousness coexist seamlessly on the open road.

76

2017 Lamborghini Terzo Millennio

Imagine a glimpse into the future, a world where the intersection of art, technology, and performance takes center stage. In this electrifying realm, the Lamborghini Terzo Millennio emerges as a beacon of innovation, a concept car that shatters the limits of imagination and propels us into a new era of automotive excellence.

Envision a moment when the boundaries between dreams and reality blur, where a car becomes not just a means of transportation, but a canvas for revolutionary ideas. In this era of transformative innovation, the Lamborghini Terzo Millennio finds its place – a creation that's not just a car, but a vision of what's possible when brilliance and imagination merge. Crafted by the ingenious minds at Lamborghini, this concept car represents a fusion of cutting-edge technology and the art of the possible.

The Terzo Millennio's design is a symphony of sharp edges and futuristic lines, a marriage of aesthetics and aerodynamics that captures both the eye's admiration and the road's embrace. Its low, aggressive stance radiates power and speed, while the signature Lamborghini hexagonal shapes and Y motifs evoke a sense of dynamism and excellence. The sleek finish, like a portal to the future, mirrors the car's essence of innovation and performance.

However, the significance of the Terzo Millennio goes beyond its captivating exterior. Beneath its stunning surface lies a world of groundbreaking technologies and engineering brilliance. This concept car showcases Lamborghini's dedication to pushing the boundaries of performance, introducing cutting-edge features like electric powertrains powered by supercapacitors and self-healing carbon fiber materials. Its blend of futuristic design and advanced technologies sets a new standard for Lamborghini's approach to creating hypercars that redefine the limits of speed and sustainability.

In 2017, the Lamborghini Terzo Millennio made its exhilarating entrance, captivating enthusiasts with its blend of form and function. While not destined for mass production, the Terzo Millennio's innovations and ideas continue to influence Lamborghini's journey towards the future. Its pioneering technologies have paved the way for the development of electric and hybrid powertrains in Lamborghini's upcoming models, reshaping the brand's approach to performance and sustainability.

As you conjure the image of the Lamborghini Terzo Millennio, let it fuel your own aspirations to fuse innovation with passion in your endeavors. Let it remind you that true greatness often involves pushing the boundaries of what's possible while maintaining an unwavering commitment to excellence. Just as the Terzo Millennio's pursuit of innovative design and engineering brilliance influenced Lamborghini's journey, so too can your audacious spirit shape the trajectory of your dreams. Its legacy isn't limited to its groundbreaking technologies or futuristic design; it's a testament to the idea that the fusion of vision, engineering, and audacity can shape industries and inspire us to accelerate towards our aspirations.

77

2017 BMW 8 Series Concept

Step into a world where innovation and elegance coalesce, where automotive dreams are sculpted into reality with precision and passion. In this captivating realm, the BMW 8 Series Concept emerges as a beacon of sophistication, a concept car that embodies the very essence of luxury and performance, and dares us to envision the future of driving.

Imagine a moment when power and grace unite in harmony, creating a car that's not just a mode of transportation, but a statement of refined excellence. In this era of automotive artistry, the BMW 8 Series Concept takes its rightful place – not just as a car, but as an embodiment of BMW's commitment to elevating the driving experience. Conceived by the masterful minds at BMW, this concept car represents a fusion of cutting-edge engineering and artistic design.

The design of the 8 Series Concept is a symphony of sleek lines and sculpted curves, a marriage of aesthetics and aerodynamics that captures both the eye's admiration and the wind's embrace. Its low, dynamic profile exudes a sense of power and luxury, while the signature BMW kidney grille and elegant lighting elements evoke a timeless sense of refinement and modernity. The polished finish, like a mirror reflecting the future, mirrors the car's essence of innovation and class.

Yet, the significance of the 8 Series Concept goes beyond its captivating exterior. Under its exquisite skin lies a world of advanced technology and engineering brilliance. This concept car showcases BMW's dedication to pushing the boundaries of performance, introducing features like carbon-fiber construction and precision-engineered drivetrains. Its blend of modern design and cutting-edge technology sets a new standard for BMW's approach to creating luxury vehicles that seamlessly blend elegance with exhilaration.

In 2017, the BMW 8 Series Concept made its grand debut, captivating enthusiasts with its blend of form and function. While not all aspects of the concept transitioned directly to production, its design philosophy and technological innovations had a profound influence on the design language and features of the mass-produced BMW 8 Series that followed. The 8 Series model reestablished BMW's presence in the luxury coupe segment and continues to set the standard for combining opulence with driving performance.

As you conjure the image of the BMW 8 Series Concept, let it ignite your own aspirations to infuse innovation with luxury in your pursuits. Let it remind you that true greatness often involves embracing the intersection of art and engineering while crafting beauty and power in perfect harmony. Just as the 8 Series Concept's pursuit of design elegance and engineering brilliance influenced BMW's journey, so too can your audacious spirit shape the trajectory of your dreams. Its legacy isn't confined to its exquisite design or advanced technologies; it's a testament to the idea that the fusion of passion, engineering, and creativity can shape industries and inspire us to accelerate towards our aspirations.

78

2017 Honda Urban EV Concept

Imagine a world where your car isn't just a machine; it's a companion, a conversation starter, and a source of joy. In this vision of the future, Honda gave us a glimpse with the Urban EV Concept.

The Honda Urban EV Concept, unveiled in 2017, is a harmonious blend of retro charm and futuristic innovation. It's as if the beloved Honda Civic from the past met a sci-fi movie set in the future and they created a new kind of automotive magic together.

What immediately catches your eye is the Urban EV's design. It exudes an inviting, friendly character with its compact dimensions, smooth curves, and a front fascia that seems to smile at you. The large digital display between the headlights doesn't just show the time; it can display messages or even offer a friendly greeting.

Stepping inside the cabin feels like entering a tech-savvy living room. The dashboard features a massive touchscreen interface that stretches across the entire width. It's not just for controlling the car; it's your portal to the world, offering everything from navigation to social media updates. The upholstery, made from environmentally friendly materials, adds to the feeling of being inside a forward-thinking, sustainable oasis.

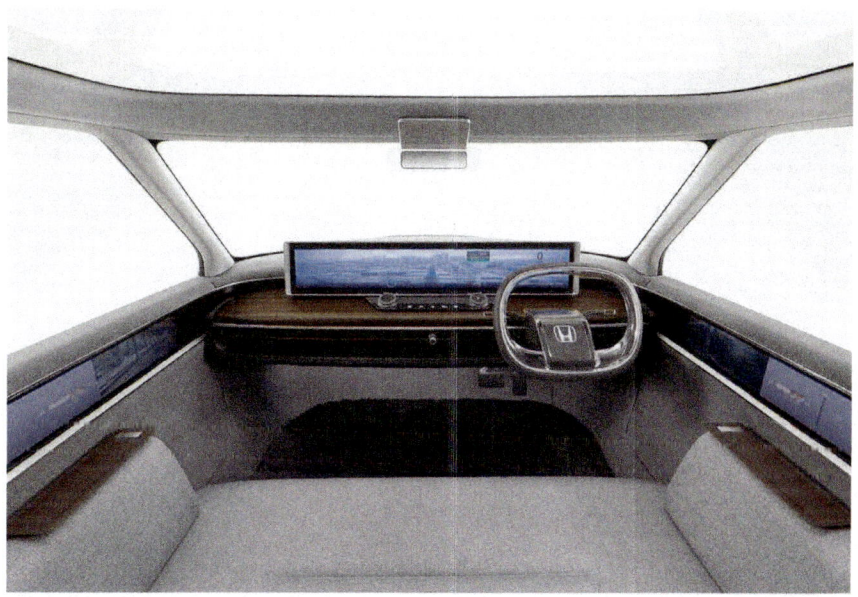

But the Urban EV Concept isn't just about looks. Underneath that charming exterior lies an all-electric powertrain. It's silent, efficient, and eco-friendly, a testament to Honda's commitment to a cleaner future. The battery technology developed for this concept will eventually find its way into Honda's production electric vehicles, contributing to a greener world.

The Urban EV Concept isn't just a car; it's a statement. It tells us that the future of mobility can be both environmentally responsible and emotionally satisfying. It's a reminder that innovation and sustainability can coexist beautifully. And it inspires us to imagine a world where our cars are not just tools but also friends, making our lives better and brighter. Honda's Urban EV Concept shows us that the future of driving is not just about getting from point A to B but about the experiences we have along the way.

79

2017 Aston Martin Valkyrie

Imagine a world where the boundaries of speed and artistry collide, birthing a machine that transcends the realm of automobiles and becomes a true work of kinetic art. In this exhilarating reality, the Aston Martin Valkyrie emerges as a symphony of innovation and performance, a concept car that not only redefines the limits of speed but also invites us to ponder the future of automotive engineering.

Envision a moment when power and design are entwined to create not just a vehicle, but a masterpiece that sings the song of velocity. In this era of automotive revolution, the Aston Martin Valkyrie takes center stage – not as a mere concept, but as a declaration of Aston Martin's unwavering commitment to pushing the envelope of driving perfection. Born from the collaboration between Aston Martin and Red Bull Advanced Technologies, this concept car represents a harmonious fusion of power and design.

The design of the Aston Martin Valkyrie is a fusion of exquisite curves and aerodynamic mastery, a choreography of aesthetics and speed that captures both the eye's wonder and the wind's embrace. Its radical proportions exude a sense of ferocity and modernity, while the distinctive bodywork and F1-inspired elements evoke a timeless sense of performance and precision. The striking color palette, like strokes of automotive genius, mirrors the car's embodiment of speed and innovation.

However, the significance of the Aston Martin Valkyrie transcends its breathtaking exterior. Beneath its stunning surface lies a symphony of advanced technology and engineering brilliance. This concept car showcases Aston Martin's dedication to pushing the boundaries of performance, introducing cutting-edge features like a naturally aspirated V12 engine with hybrid assistance. Its fusion of power and innovation sets a new standard for Aston Martin's approach to creating vehicles that redefine the art of driving.

The Aston Martin Valkyrie made its dazzling debut in 2017, capturing the hearts of enthusiasts with its blend of form and function. While not every detail of the concept transitioned directly to production, its influence reverberates through Aston Martin's lineup, guiding the development of the Aston Martin Valkyrie hypercar. The Valkyrie's legacy lives on in Aston Martin's unwavering pursuit of creating vehicles that marry raw power with exquisite design.

As you visualize the Aston Martin Valkyrie, let it ignite your aspirations to merge aesthetics with velocity in your pursuits. Let it remind you that true greatness often involves challenging the boundaries of what's achievable while embracing the allure of design. Just as the Valkyrie's pursuit of performance and artistic brilliance influenced Aston Martin's journey, so too can your audacious spirit shape the trajectory of your dreams. Its legacy isn't limited to its powerful features or visionary design; it's a testament to the idea that the fusion of passion, engineering, and performance can shape industries and inspire us to accelerate towards our aspirations.

80

2017 Volkswagen ID. BUZZ Concept

Close your eyes and picture a future where the past meets the present, where the iconic design of a beloved classic is reborn into an electrified era. In this captivating vision, the Volkswagen ID. BUZZ Concept emerges as a bridge between nostalgia and innovation, a concept car that not only pays homage to a timeless icon but also propels us toward an electrified and sustainable future.

Imagine a moment when the legendary Volkswagen Microbus is reimagined as an all-electric marvel, carrying the spirit of adventure and camaraderie into the 21st century. In this era of automotive transformation, the Volkswagen ID. BUZZ Concept takes center stage – not merely as a concept, but as a testament to Volkswagen's commitment to redefining mobility with an eco-conscious twist. Born from the iconic Microbus heritage and modern electric technology, this concept car embodies a harmonious blend of classic design and sustainable progress.

The design of the Volkswagen ID. BUZZ Concept is a delightful fusion of retro charm and cutting-edge technology, a homage to the past and a leap into the future. Its distinctive, friendly face and signature two-tone color scheme evoke a sense of nostalgia, while its clean lines and aerodynamic profile represent modernity and efficiency. The spacious interior, reminiscent of a lounge on wheels, reimagines the idea of a car cabin as a comfortable and versatile space for both passengers and drivers alike.

However, the significance of the Volkswagen ID. BUZZ Concept extends beyond its striking exterior and welcoming interior. Beneath its classic facade lies a world of advanced electric technology and engineering brilliance. This concept car showcases Volkswagen's dedication to sustainable mobility, introducing features like an all-electric powertrain and autonomous driving capabilities. Its fusion of nostalgia and innovation sets a new standard for Volkswagen's approach to creating vehicles that combine timeless design with eco-friendliness.

2017 VOLKSWAGEN ID. BUZZ CONCEPT

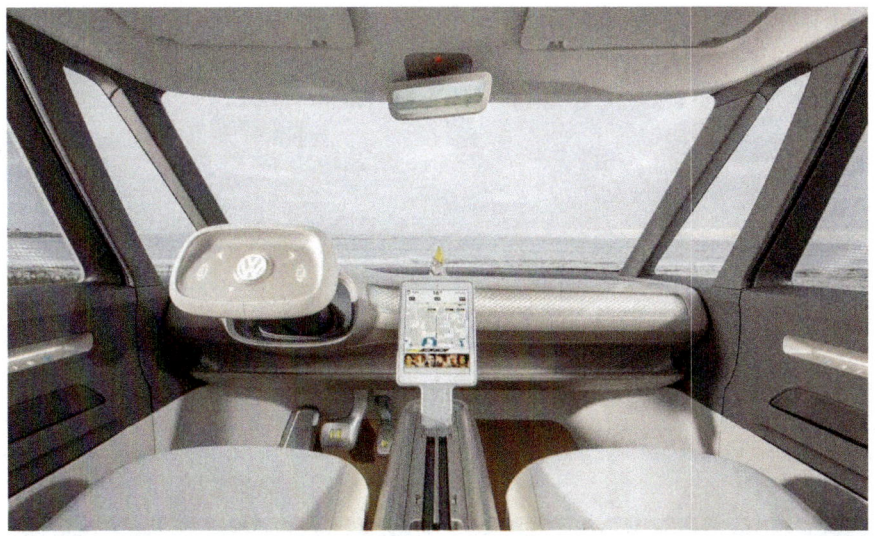

The Volkswagen ID. BUZZ Concept made its debut in 2017, captivating enthusiasts with its blend of classic aesthetics and electric prowess. Although not every detail transitioned directly to production, its influence reverberates through Volkswagen's lineup, guiding the development of electric models like the Volkswagen ID. Buzz. The ID. BUZZ Concept's legacy lives on in Volkswagen's unwavering pursuit of creating vehicles that merge heritage with sustainability.

As you envision the Volkswagen ID. BUZZ Concept, let it inspire your aspirations to blend the best of the past with the innovations of the future in your pursuits. Let it remind you that true greatness often involves paying homage to tradition while embracing the possibilities of progress. Just as the ID. BUZZ Concept's pursuit of classic design and electric innovation influenced Volkswagen's journey, so too can your audacious spirit shape the trajectory of your dreams. Its legacy isn't confined to its timeless features or visionary design; it's a testament to the idea that the fusion of passion, heritage, and sustainability can shape industries and inspire us to drive towards a greener and more connected world.

81

2017 McLaren Ultimate Vision GT

In the world of supercars, where speed meets precision, there exists a vision of pure automotive exhilaration—the McLaren Ultimate Vision GT. Imagine a car that isn't bound by the constraints of reality, a machine born from the virtual realm, and designed to push the limits of what's possible on both the racetrack and the open road.

Released in 2017 as part of the Gran Turismo video game franchise, this concept car by McLaren is a striking blend of futuristic design and cutting-edge technology. It's not just a car; it's a symphony of engineering and aesthetics, a glimpse into the future of high-performance automobiles.

The McLaren Ultimate Vision GT's design is nothing short of spectacular. Its canopy-like cockpit gives it a fighter jet-inspired appearance, and its sleek lines are optimized for aerodynamic efficiency. But what truly sets this concept car apart is its innovative technology.

Underneath its stunning exterior lies a hybrid powertrain, combining a twin-turbocharged V8 engine with an electric motor. This hybrid system delivers an astounding 1,134 horsepower, propelling the Ultimate Vision GT from 0 to 60 mph in under 2.5 seconds. It's a testament to McLaren's commitment to pushing the boundaries of speed and performance.

While the Ultimate Vision GT may exist in the virtual world, its influence on the world of supercars is very real. McLaren has taken cues from this concept car's design and technology, incorporating them into their production vehicles like the McLaren Senna and the McLaren Speedtail.

As you imagine the McLaren Ultimate Vision GT, let it inspire you to dream big, to envision a future where automotive engineering knows no bounds. It's a reminder that in the world of high-performance cars, the pursuit of perfection is a never-ending journey, where imagination and innovation fuel the road ahead. This concept car is a symbol of what's possible when dreams and technology merge, a testament to the unrelenting pursuit of automotive excellence.

82

2017 Nissan V-Motion 2.0

Picture a car that seems like it's been sculpted by the very essence of motion itself, where design meets innovation in perfect harmony—the Nissan V-Motion 2.0. This remarkable concept car embodies the spirit of Nissan's vision for the future of automotive design and technology.

2017 NISSAN V-MOTION 2.0

Unveiled at the 2017 North American International Auto Show, the V-Motion 2.0 is more than just a car; it's a rolling work of art, a statement of Nissan's commitment to pushing the boundaries of automotive aesthetics and functionality.

Its design is a testament to the art of simplicity and elegance. The V-Motion grille at the front is a striking focal point, conveying a sense of dynamic motion, while the sleek lines and fluid contours give the car an aerodynamic edge. The floating roof design, a signature of Nissan's recent innovations, adds a touch of modernity and sophistication.

But what truly sets the V-Motion 2.0 apart is the technology hidden beneath its captivating exterior. This concept car features Nissan's ProPILOT system, a precursor to their autonomous driving technology. It's a step towards a future where cars can navigate the roads with the precision of a skilled driver, making driving safer and more convenient.

While the V-Motion 2.0 itself didn't make it into mass production, its influence on Nissan's design language and technology is evident in their newer models, such as the Nissan Altima and Maxima, which have embraced elements of its sleek and dynamic design.

As you envision the Nissan V-Motion 2.0, let it inspire you to appreciate the fusion of art and technology in the world of automobiles. It's a symbol of Nissan's commitment to creating vehicles that are not just means of transportation, but expressions of style and innovation. In this concept car, the future of driving is not just practical; it's a beautiful blend of form and function.

83

2017 Audi Aicon

In the not-so-distant future, envision a world where the act of driving is transformed into a serene and luxurious experience—an experience where technology and design combine to redefine our understanding of mobility. Enter the Audi Aicon, a visionary concept car unveiled in 2017, and a glimpse into the automotive tomorrow.

The Audi Aicon is not just a car; it's a rolling sanctuary, an oasis of calm in the midst of a bustling world. Its name, derived from "AI" for artificial intelligence and "icon," perfectly encapsulates its essence. This concept car represents Audi's commitment to a future where autonomous driving reigns supreme, and the act of piloting a vehicle becomes an art form in itself.

At first glance, the Aicon exudes an aura of sophistication. With its sleek, minimalist design and striking proportions, it's a vision of what luxury could look like in the autonomous era. The absence of a traditional steering wheel and pedals is the first hint that this is not your average automobile. Instead, the Aicon invites passengers to relax in a spacious lounge-like cabin.

The interior is a symphony of premium materials and cutting-edge technology. Sumptuous seats, extravagant materials, and ambient lighting create an atmosphere of opulence. The centerpiece is a wraparound digital dashboard, offering passengers a panoramic view of information and entertainment. It's a digital cocoon where you can work, relax, or simply enjoy the ride.

But the true innovation of the Aicon lies in its autonomy. It's designed to operate at level 5 autonomy, which means it can handle all driving tasks without human intervention. It relies on a suite of sensors, cameras, and artificial intelligence to navigate the complexities of the road, making travel safer and more relaxing.

The power source of the Aicon is purely electric, showcasing Audi's commitment to sustainable mobility. With a range of over 400 miles on a single charge, it's not just eco-friendly; it's practical for long journeys.

While the Audi Aicon itself remains a concept, it has already started to influence the development of Audi's production vehicles. Elements of its design, such as the focus on autonomous driving and electric powertrains, have made their way into models like the Audi e-tron and the Audi A8, setting the stage for a future where luxury and technology seamlessly merge.

So, when you think of the Audi Aicon, envision a world where your car becomes your sanctuary, where AI and design collaborate to redefine the art of travel. It's not just a concept; it's a vision of a future where the journey becomes as enjoyable as the destination, and where the boundaries of technology and luxury are pushed to new horizons.

84

2017 Lexus LS+ Concept

Enter the world of automotive elegance and innovation with the Lexus LS+ Concept, a remarkable vehicle that stands as a testament to the brand's commitment to redefining luxury and performance. With its sleek lines and cutting-edge technologies, the Lexus LS+ Concept is not just a car; it's a glimpse into the future of transportation.

2017 LEXUS LS+ CONCEPT

Picture this: It's the year 2017, and the automotive world is abuzz with anticipation as Lexus unveils the LS+ Concept at an international auto show. As the curtains fall, the audience is greeted with a vision of automotive excellence that takes luxury and technology to an entirely new level.

At first glance, the Lexus LS+ Concept is a masterpiece of design. Its exterior is a fusion of elegance and aerodynamics, with sculpted lines that seem to be shaped by the wind itself. The sleek silhouette not only enhances its aesthetic appeal but also serves as a testament to Lexus' commitment to pushing the boundaries of design and engineering.

But it's beneath the surface where the LS+ Concept truly shines. This car is not content with merely being beautiful; it's also intelligent. At the heart of its innovation lies an advanced autonomous driving system, which represents Lexus' vision of a future where vehicles are not just tools but trusted partners in mobility.

The autonomous technology in the LS+ Concept is more than just a convenience; it's a leap toward safer and more efficient transportation. It utilizes state-of-the-art sensors, cameras, and artificial intelligence to navigate the roads with precision. Passengers can sit back, relax, and enjoy the ride, knowing that they are in the capable hands of cutting-edge technology.

The LS+ Concept is not just a fleeting glimpse of the future; it's a catalyst for change in the automotive industry. While it may not have rolled off the assembly line for mass production, its forward-thinking technologies have influenced subsequent Lexus models. Features like advanced driver-assistance systems and autonomous driving capabilities have become staples in the Lexus lineup, redefining the way we think about luxury and safety on the road.

In the world of automotive design and innovation, the Lexus LS+ Concept serves as a shining example of what's possible when a brand is unafraid to challenge the status quo. It reminds us that luxury doesn't have to be stagnant, that technology can enhance every aspect of our driving experience, and that the future of transportation is just as much about elegance as it is about efficiency. While you may not see an LS+ Concept on every street corner, its influence reverberates through every Lexus that graces the road.

85

2018 Audi PB18 e-tron

Imagine a glimpse into the future, a realm where the boundaries of innovation and artistry intertwine to create a symphony of power and elegance. In this mesmerizing world, the 2018 Audi PB18 e-tron emerges as a beacon of electrifying performance and visionary design, a concept car that transcends the ordinary and propels us into a new era of automotive brilliance.

Envision a moment when engineering prowess and aesthetic mastery unite to craft not just a car, but a work of kinetic art. In this era of electric exploration, the Audi PB18 e-tron takes its rightful place – not just as a concept, but as a testament to Audi's relentless pursuit of automotive excellence. Conceived by the visionary minds at Audi, this concept car represents a fusion of sustainable innovation and high-speed thrills.

The design of the PB18 e-tron is a ballet of sculpted surfaces and aerodynamic precision, a marriage of aesthetics and efficiency that captures both the eye's fascination and the wind's embrace. Its sleek, low-slung profile exudes a sense of speed and modernity, while the signature Audi Singleframe grille and bold lines evoke a timeless sense of dynamism and performance. The luminescent finish, like a portal to the future, reflects the car's essence of electrifying innovation.

However, the significance of the PB18 e-tron goes beyond its captivating exterior. Beneath its artful surface lies a world of cutting-edge technology and engineering brilliance. This concept car showcases Audi's dedication to pushing the boundaries of electric performance, introducing features like a solid-state battery pack and an innovative driver-centric cockpit. Its blend of sustainable power and forward-thinking design sets a new standard for Audi's approach to creating electric vehicles that redefine driving dynamics.

In 2018, the Audi PB18 e-tron made its electrifying debut, captivating enthusiasts with its blend of form and function. While not intended for mass production, the PB18 e-tron's innovations and design philosophy continue to influence Audi's journey towards electrification. Elements of its technology have been integrated into Audi's future electric models, shaping the brand's approach to electric performance and design.

As you conjure the image of the Audi PB18 e-tron, let it spark your own aspirations to combine innovation with elegance in your endeavors. Let it remind you that true greatness often involves pushing the boundaries of what's possible while maintaining an unwavering commitment to sustainability and beauty. Just as the PB18 e-tron's pursuit of innovative design and engineering brilliance influenced Audi's journey, so too can your audacious spirit shape the trajectory of your dreams. Its legacy isn't confined to its groundbreaking technologies or futuristic design; it's a testament to the idea that the fusion of passion, engineering, and vision can shape industries and inspire us to accelerate towards our aspirations.

86

2018 Mercedes-Benz Vision EQ Silver Arrow

Imagine gazing into the future of automotive excellence and finding the Mercedes-Benz Vision EQ Silver Arrow, a concept car that seems to have arrived from a realm where speed and elegance unite in perfect harmony.

Unveiled in 2018, this exceptional creation is more than just a car; it's an ode to Mercedes-Benz's storied racing history, a symbol of their commitment to a sustainable automotive future, and a masterpiece of design. The name itself conjures an image of sleek, silver perfection hurtling through time.

At first glance, the Silver Arrow is an embodiment of aerodynamic purity. Its elongated silhouette stretches like a silver streak, reminiscent of the legendary racing cars of the past. The body is a sinuous sculpture, sculpted by the wind itself, with a long, pointed nose and a streamlined rear. Every curve and contour is designed for optimal aerodynamic efficiency, as if it's poised to break the sound barrier.

The concept's interior is a blend of contemporary luxury and futuristic minimalism. A single seat, like a sleek cocoon, welcomes the driver into an environment that melds traditional materials with high-tech features. The panoramic touchscreen dashboard displays vital information and provides an immersive driving experience. This is a cockpit where the past meets the future.

But what truly sets the Vision EQ Silver Arrow apart is its powertrain. It's an all-electric concept, a glimpse into the future where sustainability meets performance. The car is powered by a massive battery pack, driving electric motors that generate an astonishing 738 horsepower. It's not just about speed; it's about doing so with zero emissions, a testament to Mercedes-Benz's dedication to environmentally responsible engineering.

2018 MERCEDES-BENZ VISION EQ SILVER ARROW

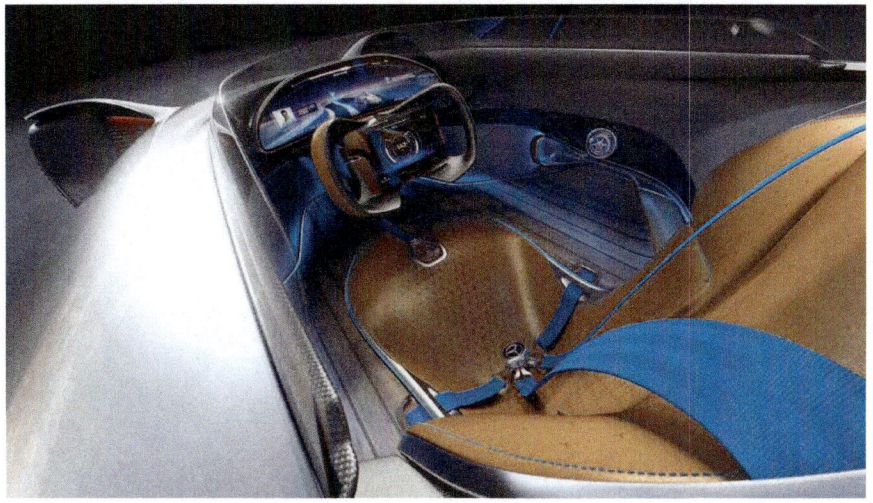

While the Vision EQ Silver Arrow remains a concept car, it has left an indelible mark on the world of luxury and performance automobiles. Mercedes-Benz took elements of its design and applied them to various mass-production models, influencing the brand's future direction. The marriage of cutting-edge electric technology with the spirit of racing heritage has set a precedent for the industry.

In summary, the Mercedes-Benz Vision EQ Silver Arrow is a manifestation of speed, elegance, and environmental responsibility. It's a reminder that automotive design can be a bridge between the past and the future, where history inspires innovation. This concept car represents Mercedes-Benz's commitment to pushing boundaries and reshaping the automotive landscape, ensuring that the pursuit of excellence never goes out of style.

87

2018 McLaren Speedtail

Picture a machine so extraordinary that it seems to have slipped from the dreams of a sci-fi visionary into our world. In this exhilarating glimpse of the future, the McLaren Speedtail emerges as a masterful blend of art and engineering, a concept car that redefines the very concept of speed and luxury, pushing the boundaries of what's possible in the world of automotive innovation.

Imagine a moment when form and function unite in perfect harmony, when the pursuit of speed and elegance becomes an obsession. In this era of automotive excellence, the McLaren Speedtail takes center stage - not just as a concept, but as a statement of McLaren's unyielding commitment to pushing the limits of performance and design. Born from the legacy of the legendary McLaren F1, this concept car embodies a harmonious fusion of speed and opulence.

The design of the McLaren Speedtail is a breathtaking testament to aerodynamic mastery and futuristic aesthetics. Its elongated, teardrop-shaped body doesn't just slice through the air; it seems to defy it. The central driving position, with two passenger seats flanking the driver, harkens back to the iconic McLaren F1, creating an intimate and immersive driving experience. The dihedral doors, which open upward and forward, are not just a show of engineering prowess but also a symbol of the car's exclusivity.

Yet, the significance of the McLaren Speedtail goes beyond its jaw-dropping exterior and bespoke interior. This concept car showcases McLaren's commitment to innovation and performance, introducing pioneering technologies like a hybrid powertrain that combines a petrol engine with electric motors, creating a staggering 1,035 horsepower. This results in a top speed of 250 mph, making it one of the fastest production cars ever.

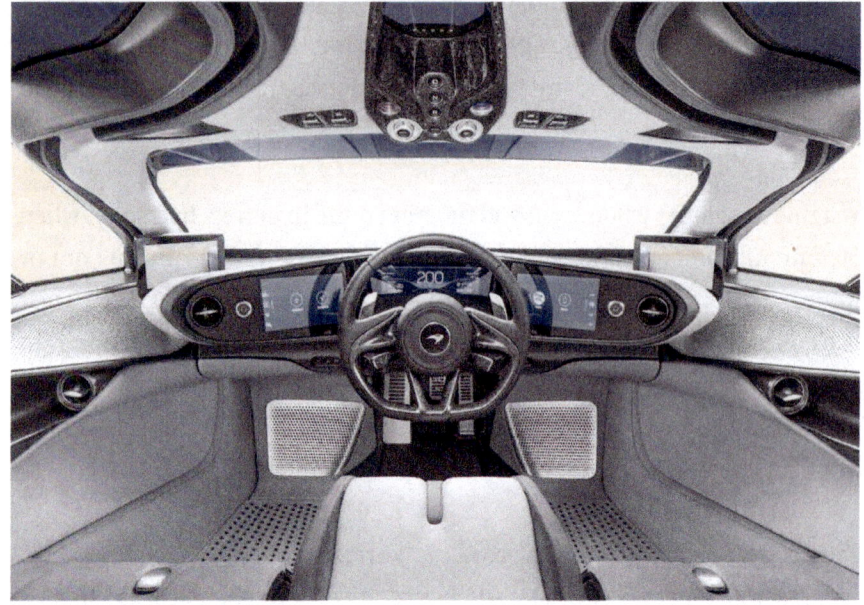

The McLaren Speedtail made its grand entrance in 2018, capturing the automotive world's attention with its extraordinary design and unmatched performance capabilities. While not every detail of the Speedtail concept made it to production, its influence can be seen in McLaren's ongoing quest for engineering excellence and speed. The concept's legacy lives on in McLaren's relentless pursuit of creating vehicles that redefine performance and luxury.

As you visualize the McLaren Speedtail, let it inspire your own pursuit of excellence and innovation in your endeavors. Let it remind you that true greatness often involves pushing the limits of what's possible while embracing the elegance of design. Just as the Speedtail's quest for speed and opulence influenced McLaren's journey, so too can your audacious spirit shape the trajectory of your dreams. Its legacy isn't confined to its remarkable features or visionary design; it's a testament to the idea that the fusion of passion, innovation, and craftsmanship can redefine industries and inspire us to move forward faster, and with more elegance, than ever before.

88

2018 Rivian R1S Concept

Buckle up for a journey into the electrifying world of the Rivian R1S Concept, an automotive masterpiece that's rewriting the story of electric adventure. Imagine a car that combines the spirit of exploration with the eco-consciousness of the modern age. That's precisely what the Rivian R1S Concept represents.

Hailing from the American electric vehicle startup, Rivian, this concept SUV made its debut in 2018 and quickly made waves across the automotive industry. It's not just a car; it's a promise of sustainable adventure that began as an audacious dream.

One look at the R1S, and you'll notice it's not your typical SUV. Its rugged and robust design cues evoke the spirit of off-road exploration, while still embodying a sleek and modern aesthetic. It's as comfortable navigating through dense forests as it is cruising downtown streets. The quad-motor setup, one at each wheel, empowers this SUV with remarkable all-wheel-drive capabilities, making it equally at home on the highway or off the beaten path.

But the Rivian R1S Concept doesn't stop at design and power. It's a showcase of innovation. The brain behind this beast is Rivian's "Skateboard" platform, where the batteries, suspension, and drivetrain are seamlessly integrated into the vehicle's floor. This unique architecture not only maximizes interior space but also provides a low center of gravity for improved stability and handling.

Step inside the R1S, and you'll find an interior that combines luxury with functionality. Sustainable materials, like wood and vegan leather, create an eco-friendly yet opulent ambiance. And there's a surprise awaiting adventure enthusiasts: the gear tunnel. Located between the rear seats and the cargo area, it's a versatile storage solution perfect for stashing snowboards, camping gear, or whatever your heart desires.

The Rivian R1S Concept has sparked a revolution in the automotive world. It's proving that electric vehicles can be more than just city commuters; they can be the adventurers' trusted companions. Its influence has spurred traditional automakers to accelerate their electric SUV plans, recognizing that sustainability and rugged capability can go hand-in-hand.

In summary, the Rivian R1S Concept is a beacon of innovation and adventure. Born in 2018, it's forging a path toward a future where eco-consciousness and exploration unite effortlessly, reminding us that the road less traveled is the one worth taking, especially when powered by electricity.

89

2019 Lamborghini V12 Vision Gran Turismo

Imagine stepping into a realm where speed and artistry unite to create a symphony of automotive excellence. In this breathtaking world, the

Lamborghini V12 Vision Gran Turismo emerges as a beacon of cutting-edge innovation and exhilarating design, a concept car that not only pushes the boundaries of performance but also inspires us to embark on a journey into the future of driving excitement.

Envision a moment when power and design genius converge to craft not just a car, but a testament to the pursuit of driving perfection. In this era of automotive ingenuity, the Lamborghini V12 Vision Gran Turismo takes center stage – not merely as a concept, but as a reflection of Lamborghini's unyielding commitment to redefining performance limits. Created by the visionary minds at Lamborghini, this concept car represents an exquisite blend of speed and artistic expression.

The design of the Lamborghini V12 Vision Gran Turismo is a marriage of sleek lines and aggressive contours, a dance of aesthetics and aerodynamics that captivates both the eye's imagination and the wind's embrace. Its dynamic proportions exude a sense of speed and modernity, while the iconic Lamborghini silhouette and distinct lighting elements evoke a timeless sense of power and performance. The vibrant finish, like a stroke of automotive artistry, reflects the car's embodiment of speed and innovation.

However, the significance of the Lamborghini V12 Vision Gran Turismo goes beyond its captivating exterior. Beneath its striking surface lies a world of advanced technology and engineering brilliance. This concept car showcases Lamborghini's dedication to pushing the boundaries of performance, introducing features like an electrified V12 powertrain and cutting-edge driving dynamics. Its fusion of speed and innovation sets a new standard for Lamborghini's approach to creating vehicles that redefine driving exhilaration.

2019 LAMBORGHINI V12 VISION GRAN TURISMO

The Lamborghini V12 Vision Gran Turismo made its grand entrance in 2019, captivating enthusiasts with its blend of form and function. Although it was designed for virtual racing in the Gran Turismo video game series, the concept's influence is unmistakable, shaping Lamborghini's approach to future performance models. The V12 Vision Gran Turismo's legacy lives on in Lamborghini's relentless pursuit of pushing the limits of speed and engineering excellence.

As you envision the Lamborghini V12 Vision Gran Turismo, let it ignite your aspirations to merge speed with artistry in your pursuits. Let it remind you that true greatness often involves daring to challenge the status quo while embracing the beauty of design. Just as the V12 Vision Gran Turismo's pursuit of speed and artistic brilliance influenced Lamborghini's journey, so too can your audacious spirit shape the trajectory of your dreams. Its legacy isn't confined to its powerful features or groundbreaking design; it's a testament to the idea that the fusion of passion, engineering, and performance can shape industries and inspire us to accelerate towards our aspirations.

90

2019 Mercedes-Benz Vision EQS

Imagine a world where elegance dances with electricity, where luxury meets sustainability in a breathtaking embrace. In this visionary realm, the Mercedes-Benz Vision EQS emerges as a symphony of innovation and opulence, a concept car that not only redefines the concept of luxury but also invites us to envision a future where driving is both environmentally conscious and exhilarating.

Envision a moment when technology and design merge to create not just a car, but a masterpiece of electric mobility. In this era of automotive transformation, the Mercedes-Benz Vision EQS takes center stage – not merely as a concept, but as a declaration of Mercedes-Benz's commitment to shaping a greener and more luxurious future. Crafted with meticulous attention to detail, this concept car embodies a harmonious blend of performance and sustainability.

The design of the Mercedes-Benz Vision EQS is a seamless fusion of elegance and aerodynamic mastery, a symphony of aesthetics and efficiency that captures both the eye's admiration and the wind's embrace. Its sweeping lines and futuristic contours exude a sense of grace and modernity, while the iconic star-studded grille and illuminated elements showcase a timeless sense of Mercedes-Benz heritage and innovation. The luxurious interior, akin to a cocoon of serenity, envelops passengers in a realm of comfort and advanced technology.

However, the significance of the Mercedes-Benz Vision EQS goes beyond its captivating exterior and opulent interior. Beneath its sleek surface lies a world of advanced electric technology and engineering brilliance. This concept car showcases Mercedes-Benz's dedication to pushing the boundaries of electric mobility, introducing features like a powerful electric drivetrain and cutting-edge battery technology. Its fusion of luxury and sustainability sets a new standard for Mercedes-Benz's approach to creating vehicles that redefine both opulence and eco-friendliness.

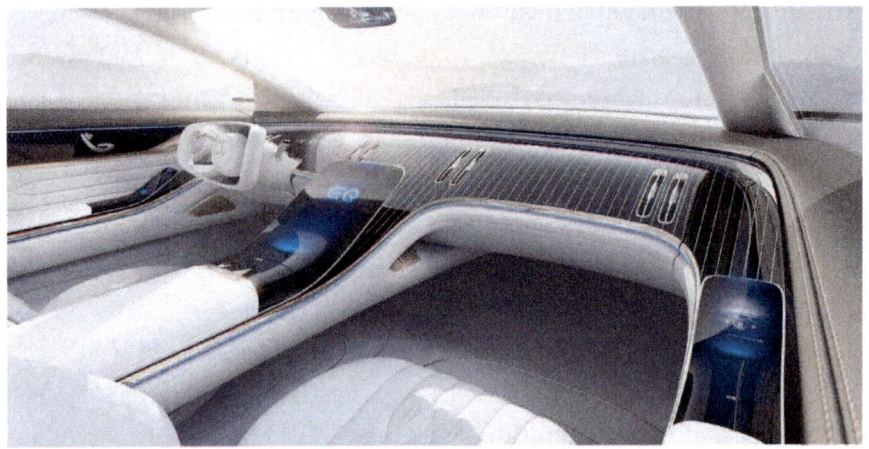

The Mercedes-Benz Vision EQS made its grand entrance in 2019, captivating the automotive world with its blend of luxury and electric performance. Although not every detail directly translated to production, its influence resonates through Mercedes-Benz's lineup, guiding the development of electric models like the Mercedes-Benz EQS. The Vision EQS's legacy lives on in Mercedes-Benz's unwavering pursuit of creating vehicles that merge luxury with environmental consciousness.

As you imagine the Mercedes-Benz Vision EQS, let it inspire your aspirations to merge luxury with sustainability in your pursuits. Let it remind you that true greatness often involves daring to reimagine possibilities while embracing the allure of design. Just as the Vision EQS's pursuit of opulence and electric brilliance influenced Mercedes-Benz's journey, so too can your audacious spirit shape the trajectory of your dreams. Its legacy isn't confined to its luxurious features or visionary design; it's a testament to the idea that the fusion of passion, engineering, and sustainability can shape industries and inspire us to drive towards a brighter future.

91

2019 Lexus LF-30 Electrified

Close your eyes and step into the future, where innovation and sustainability dance in perfect harmony. In this thrilling vision of tomorrow's mobility, the Lexus LF-30 Electrified takes center stage as a symbol of bold design, cutting-edge technology, and a commitment to a greener planet.

Picture a moment when luxury and environmental consciousness intertwine seamlessly. In this era of electric revolution, the Lexus LF-30 Electrified emerges as a masterpiece, not just as a concept car but as a testament to

Lexus's dedication to a sustainable and electrified future. Born from the marque's rich history of luxury and innovation, this concept car represents a harmonious blend of opulence and eco-friendliness.

The design of the Lexus LF-30 Electrified is a breathtaking glimpse into the future of automotive aesthetics. Its sleek, organic lines and striking angular shapes give it an otherworldly presence, a vision of what's possible when design and technology converge. The cabin is a sanctuary of opulence, blending sustainable materials and cutting-edge technology to create an environment of pure luxury.

But the LF-30's significance extends far beyond its captivating exterior and sumptuous interior. This concept car showcases Lexus's commitment to a sustainable future, introducing groundbreaking technologies like an all-electric powertrain and autonomous driving capabilities. With four in-wheel electric motors and a next-generation battery, it offers a glimpse into a world where performance and sustainability coexist.

2019 LEXUS LF-30 ELECTRIFIED

The Lexus LF-30 Electrified was unveiled in 2019, marking a pivotal moment in the luxury automaker's journey towards electrification. While not every detail of the LF-30 made it to production, its influence is evident in Lexus's continued development of electric and hybrid vehicles. The concept's legacy lives on in Lexus's unwavering pursuit of creating vehicles that combine opulence with sustainability.

As you envision the Lexus LF-30 Electrified, let it inspire your own commitment to a more sustainable and innovative future. Let it remind you that luxury doesn't have to come at the expense of our planet. Just as the LF-30's pursuit of opulence and sustainability has influenced Lexus's journey, so too can your dedication to excellence and eco-friendliness shape the trajectory of your dreams. Its legacy isn't confined to its luxurious features or visionary design; it's a testament to the idea that the fusion of luxury, technology, and sustainability can redefine industries and inspire us to move forward towards a greener and more elegant world.

92

2019 BMW Vision M Next

Imagine a car that's not just a means of transport but a thrilling embodiment of the future of driving—a glimpse into a world where performance meets sustainability, where innovation and aesthetics converge. Enter the BMW Vision M Next, a concept car that made its debut in 2019, setting the automotive world ablaze with its bold vision.

The BMW Vision M Next is not just a car; it's a declaration of intent from the Bavarian automaker. It's a marriage of cutting-edge technology and timeless design, a fusion of electrification and exhilaration. This concept car is a testament to BMW's unwavering commitment to shaping the future of mobility.

Its design is a symphony of elegance and aggression. With its wedge-shaped silhouette, the Vision M Next is a nod to BMW's legendary M1 sports car from the late '70s. The iconic kidney grille is flanked by striking laser headlights, giving the car an unmistakable presence on the road. The Vision's exterior is finished in a bold shade of Thrilling Orange, a color that's as daring as its performance.

Speaking of performance, the Vision M Next is a plug-in hybrid electric vehicle (PHEV) with a total power output of around 600 horsepower. It's capable of sprinting from 0 to 60 mph in just 3 seconds, all while offering an all-electric driving range for those eco-conscious moments.

What makes the Vision M Next truly revolutionary, however, is its focus on the driver. It features a BOOST+ mode that offers an extra surge of power, allowing you to fully immerse yourself in the thrill of driving. It's the perfect blend of sustainable electric driving and the sheer excitement of a sports car.

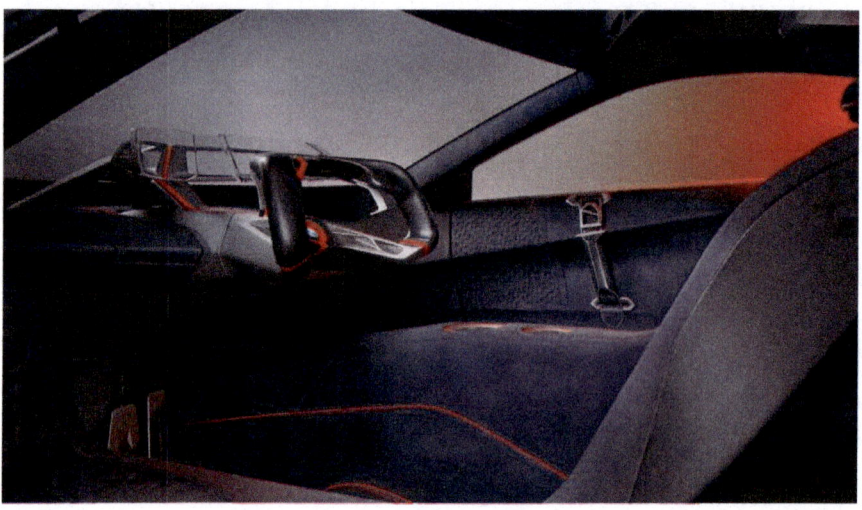

While the Vision M Next itself is a concept, its influence on BMW's production cars is profound. It's a harbinger of BMW's electrification strategy, a strategy that's led to the creation of electric vehicles like the BMW i4 and the BMW iX3. The Vision M Next is not just a car; it's a vision of the future where driving is not just about getting from point A to B but about the journey itself—a journey filled with power, precision, and a deep commitment to sustainability.

So, when you think of the BMW Vision M Next, envision a future where the joy of driving is not compromised by the need to protect our planet. It's a beacon of hope for car enthusiasts and environmentalists alike—a symbol of a world where performance and sustainability coexist in perfect harmony.

93

2019 Nissan Aria Concept

Ladies and gentlemen, let me introduce you to a glimpse of the automotive future, the Nissan Aria Concept. Imagine a car that seamlessly blends the power of electric propulsion with the elegance of a luxury sedan. The Aria Concept, born from Nissan's innovative spirit, offers precisely that and so much more.

Unveiled in 2019, the Nissan Aria Concept is not just a car; it's a vision of what's to come in the world of electric vehicles. This avant-garde creation melds cutting-edge technology with a design philosophy that hints at a harmonious coexistence with the environment.

First, let's talk about the design. The Aria Concept is a sculptural masterpiece, with flowing lines and a minimalist aesthetic. Its sleek and aerodynamic body appears to have been carved by the wind itself, demonstrating Nissan's commitment to efficiency without sacrificing style. The panoramic glass roof lets passengers bask in natural light, creating an open and inviting interior.

Now, onto the technology. The Aria Concept is fully electric, embracing Nissan's vision of a sustainable future. Its dual electric motors deliver powerful acceleration and a whisper-quiet ride, all while producing zero emissions. The concept introduced Nissan's e-4ORCE technology, a groundbreaking all-wheel-drive system that enhances stability and handling, especially in adverse weather conditions. This technology has since made its way into Nissan's production EVs, ensuring a safe and confident driving experience for all.

Step inside, and you're greeted by a cabin that feels more like a sanctuary than a car interior. Sustainable materials like recycled ocean plastic and wood sourced from forests with a commitment to sustainability adorn the cabin, highlighting Nissan's dedication to eco-conscious design.

One of the Aria Concept's most notable features is the Nissan Air Recirculation System, which uses a unique plasma filter to remove allergens and viruses from the cabin's air. This innovation, born from the need for cleaner, healthier air, has the potential to transform the way we think about interior air quality in vehicles.

2019 NISSAN ARIA CONCEPT

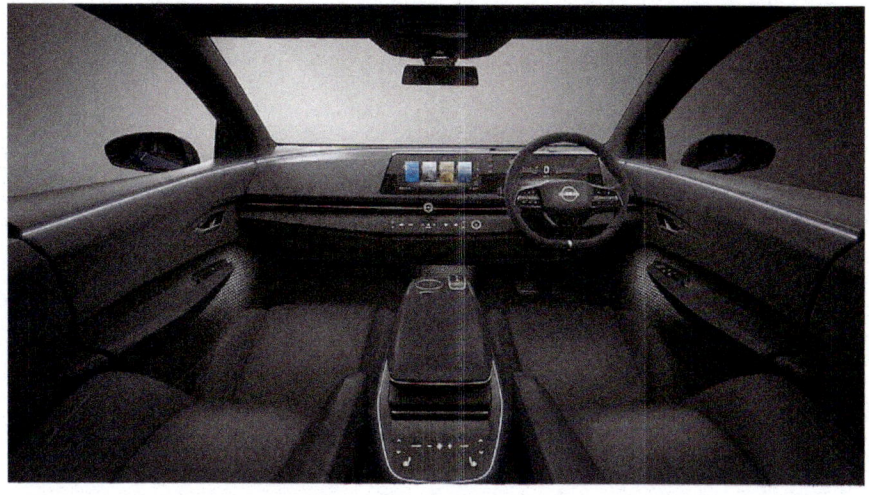

While the Aria Concept itself remains a vision of tomorrow, its influence on Nissan's electric vehicle lineup is already evident. Elements of its design, from its clean lines to its commitment to sustainability, have found their way into Nissan's production electric vehicles, making the dream of a cleaner, more connected future a reality.

In essence, the Nissan Aria Concept is not just a car; it's a statement. It's a declaration of Nissan's dedication to pushing the boundaries of what's possible, both in design and technology. It's a glimpse of the future of mobility, where elegance and innovation coexist harmoniously, where electric power is harnessed for a cleaner world, and where driving becomes an experience that transcends the ordinary.

94

2019 Aston Martin Valhalla Prototype

Imagine a car that isn't just a mode of transportation, but a symphony of engineering excellence and artistic design—a car that could only be born from the dreams of a legendary British marque. This automotive masterpiece is the Aston Martin Valhalla Prototype, a vehicle that takes you on a journey into the future of automotive luxury and performance.

2019 ASTON MARTIN VALHALLA PROTOTYPE

Released in 2019 as a prototype, the Aston Martin Valhalla is a manifestation of innovation and craftsmanship. Its name, "Valhalla," conjures images of the great hall in Norse mythology where the bravest of warriors are celebrated, and this car lives up to that legacy.

The design of the Valhalla is a poetic blend of form and function. Its low-slung, aerodynamic body seems to have been sculpted by the wind itself, with flowing lines that evoke a sense of motion even when standing still. The prominent butterfly doors give it an otherworldly appearance, like something that has landed from the future.

One of the most striking features is the car's unique roof, crafted from a single piece of carbon fiber. This not only reduces weight but also adds to its structural integrity. The interior is a work of art in itself, with a driver-focused cockpit and luxurious materials that cocoon you in comfort and style.

But it's beneath the hood and body where the Valhalla truly shines. This supercar is a hybrid, featuring a potent twin-turbocharged V6 engine coupled with an electric motor. Together, they produce over 950 horsepower, delivering heart-pounding acceleration and a top speed that pushes the boundaries of what's possible on the open road.

The Valhalla's innovative technologies extend to its aerodynamics, with an active suspension system that adjusts to provide optimal handling and ride comfort. Its performance isn't just raw power; it's a finely tuned dance of technology and artistry.

While the Valhalla itself is a rare and exclusive vehicle, its influence on the future of Aston Martin's production cars is profound. The groundbreaking technologies and design principles developed for the Valhalla are making their way into Aston Martin's mainstream models, elevating the entire brand to new heights of performance and luxury.

In essence, the Aston Martin Valhalla Prototype is not just a car; it's a testament to human ingenuity, a glimpse into the future of automotive engineering, and a work of art that inspires us to dream bigger and reach for the stars. It embodies the spirit of innovation and craftsmanship that defines the Aston Martin brand, reminding us that the future of automotive excellence is limited only by our imagination.

95

2019 Canoo Lifestyle Vehicle Concept

Imagine a car that's more than just a means of transportation. It's a canvas of innovation, a symphony of design, and a peek into a sustainable future. This is the Canoo Lifestyle Vehicle Concept.

In the recent wave of electric vehicles, Canoo has emerged as a trailblazer, redefining what we expect from automobiles. Their Lifestyle Vehicle Concept, unveiled in 2019, challenged conventional notions of car design and function.

What immediately sets the Canoo concept apart is its unconventional shape. It's neither a sedan nor an SUV, but a fresh interpretation of mobility. The cabin is spacious, with a lounge-like interior that invites passengers to relax and socialize. It's a departure from the traditional driver-focused cockpit, emphasizing shared experiences and connectivity.

But it's beneath the surface where the Canoo truly shines. The vehicle is fully electric, part of Canoo's vision for a cleaner, greener future. What's groundbreaking is their unique skateboard platform, housing the battery and electric drivetrain. This modular platform can be adapted for various vehicle types, from delivery vans to personal cars, making it a versatile solution for future mobility.

Canoo's Lifestyle Vehicle Concept sparked a shift in how we think about cars. It challenged the idea that each person needs a private vehicle, suggesting that shared mobility could be the way forward. This shift towards more efficient, sustainable, and shared transportation has influenced the automotive industry, with other companies exploring similar concepts.

In essence, the Canoo Lifestyle Vehicle Concept isn't just a car; it's a revolution on wheels. It's a reminder that the future of mobility is not only electric but also reimagined for a world that values sustainability and shared experiences. Canoo has shown us that the road ahead is not just about getting from place to place; it's about getting there together, in style and with a commitment to a brighter, cleaner tomorrow.

96

2019 Bentley EXP 100 GT

Imagine stepping into a realm of automotive luxury like no other, where elegance meets innovation, and tradition embraces the future. In the year 2019, Bentley, the epitome of British craftsmanship, unveiled a concept car that not only turned heads but redefined what grand touring could be – the Bentley EXP 100 GT.

2019 BENTLEY EXP 100 GT

The Bentley EXP 100 GT is a masterpiece of design and engineering, a testament to the brand's commitment to creating the most exquisite automobiles. It's more than just a car; it's a bold vision for the next century of grand touring. As you delve into its story, you'll understand why it's become an iconic symbol of automotive excellence.

Picture a car that exudes opulence from every angle. The EXP 100 GT boasts a captivating exterior design, blending timeless Bentley aesthetics with futuristic touches. Its long, sweeping lines, illuminated grille, and intricate details pay homage to Bentley's rich heritage, while its cutting-edge technology and sustainable materials point toward the future of luxury.

But it's not just about appearances; the EXP 100 GT reimagines the driving experience. This concept car showcases the future of sustainable mobility with an all-electric powertrain, a nod to Bentley's commitment to environmental responsibility. It offers a range of innovative technologies, such as an AI-driven "Bentley Personal Assistant" that anticipates your needs and desires.

Step inside the EXP 100 GT, and you're enveloped in a world of unparalleled luxury. The cabin is a sanctuary of sustainable materials like organic leather and British wool, creating an eco-conscious yet sumptuous environment. It's designed to offer an immersive driving experience while emphasizing the importance of well-being.

Released as part of Bentley's centenary celebrations, the EXP 100 GT goes beyond being a concept; it's a blueprint for the future of grand touring. It influences the way Bentley and other luxury automakers approach sustainability, craftsmanship, and the fusion of tradition with innovation.

In essence, the Bentley EXP 100 GT invites us to dream about the future of automotive opulence. It's a beacon of inspiration for a world where luxury not only embraces technology but also takes responsibility for the planet. This concept car embodies the spirit of Bentley's heritage while driving us toward a new era of sustainable extravagance.

97

2020 Mercedes-Benz Vision AVTR

Step into the future of mobility with the Mercedes-Benz Vision AVTR, a concept car that feels like it's been plucked from a science fiction universe and brought to life. Inspired by the iconic movie "Avatar," this visionary vehicle is a testament to the boundless imagination and innovation that Mercedes-Benz brings to the automotive world.

Imagine a car that blurs the lines between man and machine, nature and technology. The Vision AVTR is a symphony of organic design and futuristic technology, designed to coexist harmoniously with the world around it. Its name, AVTR, stands for "Advanced Vehicle Transformation," and it's not just a car; it's a living, breathing entity.

Released in 2020, the Vision AVTR is a rolling showcase of Mercedes-Benz's commitment to sustainable, eco-friendly mobility. It's powered by a groundbreaking electric drivetrain, with batteries made from recyclable materials. The vehicle is also designed to give back to nature, with a unique feature that allows it to interact with the environment, almost like a living organism.

The design of the Vision AVTR is a masterpiece in itself. Its shape is inspired by the elegant silhouette of a wild animal, with a stretched, sleek profile that mimics the muscular grace of a feline predator. The exterior is covered in thousands of tiny, light-sensitive scales that respond to touch and gesture, adding an element of interactivity and a sense of connection between the driver and the vehicle.

But what truly sets the Vision AVTR apart is its innovative "One With Nature" concept. The car is equipped with biometric sensors that can read the driver's pulse and breathing, creating a unique and symbiotic connection between human and machine. It even features a "control center" in the center console, which can be operated with a simple hand gesture.

Inside the Vision AVTR, you'll find a cabin that feels more like a luxurious lounge than a car interior. Sustainable materials abound, and the seats seem to float within the cabin, creating an ethereal, weightless feeling. The dashboard is a massive curved screen that displays vital information and can be customized to suit the driver's preferences.

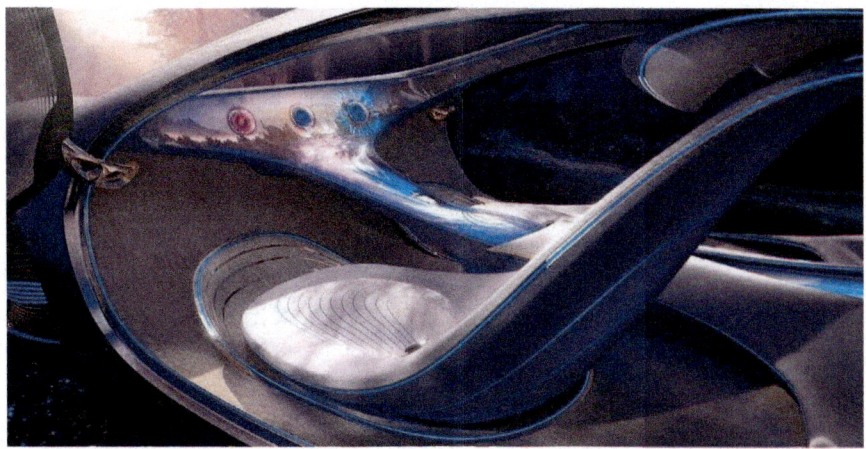

While the Mercedes-Benz Vision AVTR has yet to become a mass-produced vehicle, its influence is already profound. It's a shining example of the direction the automotive industry is moving, with a focus on sustainability, eco-conscious materials, and a reimagining of the relationship between driver and machine. The technologies and design cues seen in the AVTR are likely to find their way into future Mercedes-Benz production vehicles, making the future of driving not just electric but also more in tune with nature and more connected to the driver's own physiology.

The Vision AVTR is not just a concept car; it's a vision of what the future of mobility could be—a future where innovation and sustainability go hand in hand, where the car is not just a mode of transport but a partner in the journey, and where the lines between human and machine blur in the most beautiful and profound ways.

98

2021 Audi RS Q e-tron

Ladies and gentlemen, fasten your seatbelts and prepare to be awed by the groundbreaking Audi RS Q e-tron, a concept car that redefines the very essence of off-road racing. Imagine a vehicle so advanced, so forward-thinking, that it could conquer the most grueling terrains on Earth while emitting nothing but electric whispers.

Born from Audi's unyielding commitment to innovation, the RS Q e-tron was unveiled in 2021 as Audi's audacious entry into the Dakar Rally, one of the most demanding motorsport events on the planet. But it's not just another race car; it's a testament to Audi's vision of sustainable, high-performance driving.

At first glance, the RS Q e-tron appears as though it's descended from the distant future. Its sleek, muscular lines and aggressive stance hint at the immense power lurking within. But the real magic lies under the skin. This concept car is powered by a cutting-edge electric powertrain, featuring a high-voltage battery and an innovative energy recuperation system.

What truly sets the RS Q e-tron apart is its unique energy strategy. Instead of relying solely on charging stations, it employs a range extender concept, a powerful TFSI engine, to charge the battery while on the go. This innovation allows it to cover long distances without the need for frequent pit stops, a game-changing approach to electric racing.

The RS Q e-tron's four electric motors, one on each wheel, provide jaw-dropping acceleration and traction that's unparalleled in the world of off-road racing. Its quattro all-wheel-drive system ensures that power is delivered precisely to where it's needed, making it a force to be reckoned with on any terrain.

Influence? Oh, it has had quite an impact. While the RS Q e-tron is a concept car, its technology and design philosophy have already begun to trickle down into Audi's production models. It's a reminder that Audi is dedicated to pushing the boundaries of what's possible, not only on the racetrack but also on the road.

So, the Audi RS Q e-tron isn't just a concept car; it's a glimpse into a greener, more electrifying future of motorsport. It's a testament to Audi's relentless pursuit of excellence, pushing the envelope of electric vehicle technology while conquering the toughest terrains the world has to offer. It's a reminder that the future of racing isn't just about speed; it's about sustainability and innovation, and Audi is leading the way.

99

2021 Genesis X Concept

Imagine a glimpse into the future of automotive elegance, where artistry and innovation converge to create a symphony of design and technology. In this visionary landscape, the Genesis X Concept emerges as a beacon of luxury and forward-thinking design, a concept car that not only redefines the boundaries of automotive aesthetics but also inspires us to reimagine the essence of luxury driving.

Envision a moment when style and engineering brilliance intertwine to craft not just a vehicle, but an embodiment of modern sophistication. In this era of automotive evolution, the Genesis X Concept takes center stage – not merely as a concept, but as a testament to Genesis's unwavering commitment to elevating the luxury experience. Conceived by the ingenious minds at Genesis, this concept car represents a harmonious blend of artistic elegance and cutting-edge technology.

The design of the Genesis X Concept is a marriage of sleek lines and sculpted contours, a ballet of aesthetics and aerodynamics that captures both the eye's admiration and the wind's caress. Its bold proportions exude a sense of presence and modernity, while the signature Genesis Crest Grille and distinctive lighting elements evoke a timeless sense of prestige and refinement. The flawless finish, like a brushstroke of automotive artistry, mirrors the car's embodiment of sophistication and innovation.

However, the significance of the Genesis X Concept transcends its captivating exterior. Beneath its exquisite surface lies a world of advanced technology and engineering brilliance. This concept car showcases Genesis's dedication to pushing the boundaries of luxury, introducing features like electric powertrains and futuristic driving assistance systems. Its fusion of opulent comfort and cutting-edge innovation sets a new standard for Genesis's approach to creating vehicles that redefine modern luxury.

2021 GENESIS X CONCEPT

In 2021, the Genesis X Concept graced the stage, captivating enthusiasts with its blend of form and function. While not every detail will directly translate to production, the concept's influence resonates through Genesis's lineup, influencing the brand's design language and guiding the development of future luxury models. The Genesis X Concept's legacy lives on in the brand's pursuit of elevating the luxury driving experience.

As you envision the Genesis X Concept, let it kindle your aspirations to merge artistry with innovation in your pursuits. Let it remind you that true greatness often involves pushing the boundaries of what's possible while honoring a commitment to elegance and luxury. Just as the Genesis X Concept's pursuit of artistic design and engineering brilliance influenced Genesis's journey, so too can your audacious spirit shape the trajectory of your dreams. Its legacy isn't confined to its luxurious features or visionary design; it's a testament to the idea that the fusion of passion, engineering, and sophistication can shape industries and inspire us to accelerate towards our aspirations.

100

2021 Audi Skysphere

Close your eyes and envision a world where the boundaries between car and driver fade into the horizon, where the very essence of mobility transforms into an awe-inspiring work of art. In this visionary landscape, the Audi Skysphere emerges as a testament to the limitless possibilities of the future, where technology, design, and the thrill of the open road converge.

2021 AUDI SKYSPHERE

Imagine a moment when automotive craftsmanship transcends convention and delves into the realm of pure artistry. In this age of electrification and autonomous driving, the Audi Skysphere stands as a symbol of Audi's unwavering commitment to innovation and luxury. Born from a heritage of engineering excellence, this concept car is a beacon of transformation.

The design of the Audi Skysphere is a breathtaking glimpse into the automotive aesthetics of tomorrow. Its elegant, elongated lines and seamless surfaces evoke a sense of timeless beauty, where the lines between vehicle and sculpture blur. The interior is a sanctuary of luxury, where materials of the highest quality meet cutting-edge technology to create an environment of pure indulgence.

Yet, the Audi Skysphere's significance reaches far beyond its captivating exterior and sumptuous interior. This concept car introduces groundbreaking technologies like Level 4 autonomous driving and an electric powertrain, reimagining the driving experience. But its most remarkable feature is its transformative ability, allowing it to switch between a grand touring roadster and an autonomous city cruiser with a push of a button.

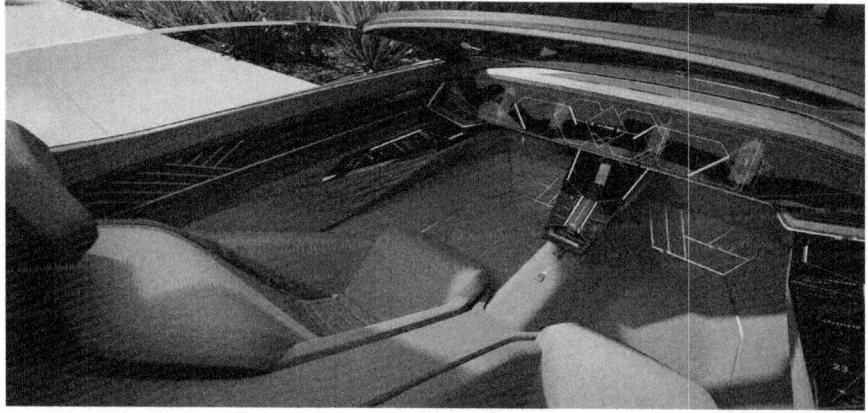

Unveiled in 2021 as part of Audi's vision for the future, the Skysphere marks a pivotal moment in the company's history, signaling a shift towards electrification and autonomous driving. While not every aspect of the Skysphere may find its way into production, its influence is evident in Audi's ongoing commitment to pushing the boundaries of innovation and luxury.

As you picture the Audi Skysphere, let it ignite your own desire for a future where technology, artistry, and the joy of driving coalesce in perfect harmony. Let it remind you that innovation need not come at the expense of luxury, and that the fusion of craftsmanship and cutting-edge technology can redefine the automotive landscape. Its legacy is not confined to its exquisite design or groundbreaking features; it's a testament to the idea that the future of mobility is a canvas upon which we can paint our dreams, where the road ahead is limited only by the boundaries of our imagination.

Printed in Great Britain
by Amazon